THE CHRISTIAN YEAR

Calendar, Lectionary and Collects

THE
CHRISTIAN YEAR

Calendar, Lectionary and Collects

 CHURCH HOUSE
PUBLISHING

Published by Church House Publishing,
Church House, Great Smith Street,
London SW1P 3NZ

Authorized edition first published 1997

ISBN 0 7151 3799 9

The Central Board of Finance is indebted to the Churches, societies, publishers and individuals whose copyright texts have been included in *Calendar, Lectionary and Collects*, either in original or in adapted form. For details see Source and Copyright Information.

Editorial, cover and page design by AD Publishing Services
Printed in England by Halstan & Co. Ltd

The Christian year, with its cycle of seasons, provides the Church with its most compelling way into the mystery of faith. The scriptures that tell the story of salvation, and the prayers proper to each week and festival, provide an annual framework for all our liturgical celebrations.

That is why in the process of revising the Church of England's contemporary material, the revision of *Calendar, Lectionary and Collects* has been undertaken before the revision of individual services. This provision is authorized from the First Sunday of Advent 1997. For three years it will provide a second alternative to *The Book of Common Prayer* and *The Alternative Service Book 1980*. Thereafter it is expected that it will replace the ASB material.

The Calendar relates to *The Book of Common Prayer* and the current practice of other Churches. At the heart of the lectionary provision is the international and ecumenical Revised Common Lectionary. The collects and post communion prayers have been agreed among the Anglican provinces in the British Isles.

THE
CALENDAR

Sundays

All Sundays celebrate the paschal mystery of the death and resurrection of the Lord. Nevertheless, they also reflect the character of the seasons in which they are set.

Principal Feasts

The principal feasts which are to be observed are:

> Christmas Day
> The Epiphany
> The Presentation of Christ in the Temple
> The Annunciation of our Lord to the Blessed Virgin Mary
> Easter Day
> Ascension Day
> Pentecost (Whit Sunday)
> Trinity Sunday
> All Saints' Day

On these days the Holy Communion is celebrated in every cathedral and parish church, and this celebration, required by Canon B 14, may only be dispensed with in accordance with the provision of Canon B 14 A.

These days, and the liturgical provision for them, may not be displaced by any other celebration, except that the Annunciation, falling on a Sunday, is transferred to the Monday following or, falling between Palm Sunday and the Second Sunday of Easter inclusive, is transferred to the Monday after the Second Sunday of Easter.

Except in the case of Christmas Day and Easter Day, the celebration of the feast begins with Evening Prayer on the day before the feast, and the collect at that Evening Prayer is that of the feast. In the case of Christmas Eve and Easter Eve, there is proper liturgical provision, including a collect, for the Eve, and this is used at both Morning and Evening Prayer.

In any year when there is a Second Sunday of Christmas, the Epiphany (6 January) may, for pastoral reasons, be celebrated on that Sunday.

The Presentation of Christ in the Temple (Candlemas) is celebrated either on 2 February or on the Sunday falling between 28 January and 3 February.

All Saints' Day is celebrated on either 1 November or the Sunday falling between 30 October and 5 November; if the latter there may be a secondary celebration on 1 November.

Other Principal Holy Days

Ash Wednesday and Maundy Thursday are principal holy days. On both these days the Holy Communion is celebrated in every cathedral or parish church, except where there is dispensation under Canon B 14 A.

Good Friday is a principal holy day.

These days, and the liturgical provision for them, may not be displaced by any other celebration.

Eastertide

The paschal character of the Great Fifty Days of Eastertide, from Easter Day to Pentecost, should be celebrated throughout the season, and should not be displaced by other celebrations. Except for a patronal or dedication festival, no festival may displace the celebration of Sunday as a memorial of the resurrection, and no saint's day may be celebrated in Easter Week.

The paschal character of the season should be retained on those weekdays when saints' days are celebrated.

Rogation Days are the three days before Ascension Day, when prayer is offered for God's blessing on the fruits of the earth and on human labour.

The nine days after Ascension Day until Pentecost are days of prayer and preparation to celebrate the outpouring of the Spirit.

Festivals

The festivals are:

The Naming and Circumcision of Jesus *(1 January)*
The Baptism of Christ
  (Epiphany 1 or, when 6 January is a Sunday, on 7 January)
The Conversion of Paul *(25 January)*
Joseph of Nazareth *(19 March)*
George, Martyr, Patron of England *(23 April)*
Mark the Evangelist *(25 April)*
Philip and James, Apostles *(1 May)*
Matthias the Apostle *(14 May)*
The Visit of the Blessed Virgin Mary to Elizabeth *(31 May)*
Barnabas the Apostle *(11 June)*
The Birth of John the Baptist *(24 June)*
Peter and Paul, Apostles *(29 June)*
Thomas the Apostle *(3 July)*
Mary Magdalene *(22 July)*
James the Apostle *(25 July)*
The Transfiguration of our Lord *(6 August)*
The Blessed Virgin Mary *(15 August)*
Bartholomew the Apostle *(24 August)*
Holy Cross Day *(14 September)*
Matthew, Apostle and Evangelist *(21 September)*
Michael and All Angels *(29 September)*
Luke the Evangelist *(18 October)*
Simon and Jude, Apostles *(28 October)*
Christ the King *(Sunday next before Advent)*
Andrew the Apostle *(30 November)*
Stephen, Deacon, First Martyr *(26 December)*
John, Apostle and Evangelist *(27 December)*
The Holy Innocents *(28 December)*

These days, and the liturgical provision for them, are not usually displaced. For each day there is full liturgical provision for the Holy Communion and for Morning and Evening Prayer.

Provision is also made for a first Evening Prayer on the day before the festival where this is required.

Festivals falling on a Sunday may be kept on that day or transferred to the Monday (or, at the discretion of the minister, to the next suitable weekday). But a festival may not be celebrated on Sundays in Advent, Lent or Eastertide. Festivals coinciding with a Principal Feast or Principal Holy Day are transferred to the first available day.

The Baptism of Christ is only transferred when 6 January is a Sunday.

Christ the King is never transferred.

When St Joseph's Day falls between Palm Sunday and the Second Sunday of Easter inclusive, it is transferred to the Monday after the Second Sunday of Easter or, if the Annunciation has already been moved to that date, to the Tuesday following.

When St George's Day or St Mark's Day fall between Palm Sunday and the Second Sunday of Easter inclusive, it is transferred to the Monday after the Second Sunday of Easter. If both fall in this period, St George's Day is transferred to the Monday and St Mark's Day to the Tuesday.

The festival of the Blessed Virgin Mary (15 August) may, for pastoral reasons, be celebrated instead on 8 September.

The Thursday after Trinity Sunday may be observed as the Day of Thanksgiving for the Holy Communion (sometimes known as Corpus Christi), and may be kept as a festival.

Local Celebrations

The celebration of the patron saint or the title of a church is kept either as a festival or as a principal feast.

The Dedication Festival of a church is the anniversary of the date of its dedication or consecration. This is kept either as a festival or as a principal feast.

When the date of dedication is unknown, the Dedication Festival may be observed on the first Sunday in October, or on the Last Sunday after Trinity, or on a suitable date chosen locally.

When kept as principal feasts, the Patronal and Dedication Festivals may be transferred to the nearest Sunday, unless that day is already a principal feast or one of the following days: The First Sunday of Advent, The Baptism of Christ, The First Sunday of Lent, The Fifth Sunday of Lent or Palm Sunday.

Harvest Thanksgiving may be celebrated on a Sunday and may replace the propers for that day, provided it does not supersede any principal feast or festival.

In the calendar of the saints, diocesan and other local provision may be made to supplement the national calendar.

Lesser Festivals

Lesser festivals, which are listed in the calendar, are observed at the level appropriate to a particular church. Each is provided with a collect, psalm and readings, which may supersede the collect of the week and the daily eucharistic lectionary. The daily psalms and readings at Morning and Evening Prayer are not usually superseded by those for lesser festivals, but at the minister's discretion psalms and readings provided on these days for the Holy Communion may be used at Morning and Evening Prayer.

The minister may be selective in the lesser festivals that are observed, and may also keep some or all of them as 'commemorations'.

When a lesser festival falls on a principal feast or holy day or on a festival, its celebration is normally omitted for that year, but, where there is sufficient reason, it may, at the discretion of the minister, be celebrated on the nearest available day.

Commemorations

Commemorations, which are listed in the calendar, are made by a mention in prayers of intercession and thanksgiving. They are not provided with collect, psalm and readings, and do not replace the usual weekday provision at either the Holy Communion or Morning and Evening Prayer.

The minister may be selective in the commemorations that are made.

A commemoration may be observed as a lesser festival, with liturgical provision from the common material for holy men and women, only where there is an established celebration in the wider church or where the day has a special local significance. In designating a commemoration as a 'lesser festival', the minister must remember the need not to lose the spirit of the season, especially of Advent and Lent, by too many celebrations that detract from its character.

Days of Discipline and Self Denial

The weekdays of Lent and every Friday in the year are days of discipline and self denial, except all principal feasts and festivals outside Lent and Fridays from Easter Day to Pentecost.

The eves of principal feasts are also appropriately kept as days of discipline and self denial in preparation for the feast.

Ember Days

Ember Days should be kept, under the bishop's directions, in the week before an ordination as days of prayer for those to be made deacon or priest.

Ember Days may also be kept even when there is no ordination in the diocese as more general days of prayer for those who serve the Church in its various ministries, both ordained and lay, and for vocations.

Traditionally they have been observed on the Wednesdays, Fridays and Saturdays within the weeks before the Third Sunday of Advent, the Second Sunday of Lent and the Sundays nearest to 29 June and 29 September.

Ordinary Time

Ordinary time is the period after the Feast of the Presentation of Christ until Shrove Tuesday, and from the day after the Feast of Pentecost until the day before the First Sunday of Advent. During ordinary time, there is no seasonal emphasis, except that the period between All Saints' Day and the First Sunday of Advent is observed as a time to celebrate and reflect upon the reign of Christ in earth and heaven.

Liturgical Colours

Appropriate liturgical colours are suggested: they are not mandatory and traditional or local use may be followed.

White is the colour for the festal periods from Christmas Day to the Presentation and from Easter Day to the Eve of Pentecost, for Trinity Sunday, for festivals of Our Lord and the Blessed Virgin Mary, for All Saints' Day, and for the festivals of those saints not venerated as martyrs, for the Feast of Dedication of a church, at Holy Communion on Maundy Thursday and in thanksgiving for Holy Communion and Holy Baptism. It is used for Marriages, and is suitable for Baptism, Confirmation and Ordination, though red may be preferred. It may be used in preference to purple or black for Funerals, and should be used at the Funeral of a Child. Where a church has two sets of white, one may be kept for great festivals indicated as 'gold or white'.

Red is used during Holy Week (except at Holy Communion on Maundy Thursday), on the Feast of Pentecost, may be used between All Saints' Day and the First Sunday of Advent (except where other provision is made) and is used for the feasts of those saints venerated as martyrs. It is appropriate for any services which focus on the gift of the Holy Spirit, and is therefore suitable for Baptism, Confirmation and Ordination.

Purple (which may vary from 'Roman purple' to violet, with blue as an alternative) is the colour for Advent and from Ash Wednesday until the day before Palm Sunday. It is recommended for Funerals and for the Commemoration of the Faithful Departed, although either black or white may be preferred. A Lent array of unbleached linen is sometimes used as an alternative to purple, but only from Ash Wednesday until the day before Palm Sunday.

Rose-colour is sometimes used as an alternative on the Third Sunday of Advent and the Fourth Sunday of Lent.

Green is used from the day after the Presentation until Shrove Tuesday, and from the day after Pentecost until the eve of All Saints' Day, except when other provision is made. It may also be used, rather than red, between All Saints' Day and the First Sunday of Advent.

Coloured hangings are traditionally removed for Good Friday and Easter Eve, but red is the colour for the liturgy on Good Friday.

The colour for a particular service should reflect the predominant theme. If the collect, readings, etc. on a lesser festival are those of the saint, then either red (for a martyr) or white is used; otherwise, the colour of the season is retained.

Typography

In the printing of the Calendar, Principal Feasts and other Principal Holy Days are printed in **BOLD UPPER CASE**; Festivals are printed in **Bold** typeface; other Sundays and Lesser Festivals are printed in ordinary roman typeface, in black. Commemorations are printed in a smaller typeface in *italics*.

Advent

The First Sunday of Advent
The Second Sunday of Advent
The Third Sunday of Advent
From 17 December (O Sapientia) *begin the eight days of prayer before Christmas Day*
The Fourth Sunday of Advent
Christmas Eve

Christmas

CHRISTMAS DAY – *25 December*
The First Sunday of Christmas
The Second Sunday of Christmas
The days after Christmas Day until the Epiphany traditionally form a unity of days of special thanksgiving

Epiphany

THE EPIPHANY – *6 January*
The Baptism of Christ – *The First Sunday of Epiphany*
The Second Sunday of Epiphany
The Third Sunday of Epiphany
The Fourth Sunday of Epiphany
THE PRESENTATION OF CHRIST IN THE TEMPLE (CANDLEMAS)
2 February

Ordinary Time

This begins on the day following The Presentation
The Fifth Sunday before Lent
The Fourth Sunday before Lent
The Third Sunday before Lent
The Second Sunday before Lent
The Sunday next before Lent

Lent

ASH WEDNESDAY
The First Sunday of Lent
The Second Sunday of Lent
The Third Sunday of Lent
The Fourth Sunday of Lent – *Mothering Sunday*
The Fifth Sunday of Lent *(Passiontide begins)*
Palm Sunday
Monday of Holy Week
Tuesday of Holy Week

Wednesday of Holy Week
MAUNDY THURSDAY
GOOD FRIDAY
Easter Eve

Easter

EASTER DAY
Monday of Easter Week
Tuesday of Easter Week
Wednesday of Easter Week
Thursday of Easter Week
Friday of Easter Week
Saturday of Easter Week
The Second Sunday of Easter
The Third Sunday of Easter
The Fourth Sunday of Easter
The Fifth Sunday of Easter
The Sixth Sunday of Easter
ASCENSION DAY
From Friday after Ascension Day begin the nine days of prayer before Pentecost
The Seventh Sunday of Easter – *Sunday after Ascension Day*
PENTECOST (Whit Sunday)

Ordinary Time

This is resumed on the Monday following the Day of Pentecost
TRINITY SUNDAY
The Day of Thanksgiving for the Institution of Holy Communion –
Thursday after Trinity Sunday (Corpus Christi)
The First Sunday after Trinity
The Second Sunday after Trinity
The Third Sunday after Trinity
The Fourth Sunday after Trinity
The Fifth Sunday after Trinity
The Sixth Sunday after Trinity
The Seventh Sunday after Trinity
The Eighth Sunday after Trinity
The Ninth Sunday after Trinity
The Tenth Sunday after Trinity
The Eleventh Sunday after Trinity
The Twelfth Sunday after Trinity
The Thirteenth Sunday after Trinity
The Fourteenth Sunday after Trinity
The Fifteenth Sunday after Trinity
The Sixteenth Sunday after Trinity
The Seventeenth Sunday after Trinity
The Eighteenth Sunday after Trinity
The Nineteenth Sunday after Trinity
The Twentieth Sunday after Trinity
The Twenty-First Sunday after Trinity
The Last Sunday after Trinity

Dedication Festival – *The First Sunday in October or The Last Sunday after Trinity if date unknown*
ALL SAINTS' DAY – *1 November*
The Sunday following 1 November may be kept as All Saints' Sunday *or as:*
The Fourth Sunday before Advent
The Third Sunday before Advent
The Second Sunday before Advent
Christ the King – *The Sunday next before Advent*

Year	Ash Wednesday	EASTER DAY
1997	12 February	30 March
1998	25 February	12 April
1999	17 February	4 April
2000	8 March	23 April
2001	28 February	15 April
2002	13 February	31 March
2003	5 March	20 April
2004	25 February	11 April
2005	9 February	27 March
2006	1 March	16 April
2007	21 February	8 April
2008	6 February	23 March
2009	25 February	12 April
2010	17 February	4 April
2011	9 March	24 April
2012	22 February	8 April
2013	13 February	31 March
2014	5 March	20 April
2015	18 February	5 April
2016	10 February	27 March
2017	1 March	16 April
2018	14 February	1 April
2019	6 March	21 April
2020	26 February	12 April
2021	17 February	4 April
2022	2 March	17 April
2023	22 February	9 April
2024	14 February	31 March
2025	5 March	20 April

Ascension Day	Pentecost (Whit Sunday)	Advent Sunday
8 May	18 May	30 November
21 May	31 May	29 November
13 May	23 May	28 November
1 June	11 June	3 December
24 May	3 June	2 December
9 May	19 May	1 December
29 May	8 June	30 November
20 May	30 May	28 November
5 May	15 May	27 November
25 May	4 June	3 December
17 May	27 May	2 December
1 May	11 May	30 November
21 May	31 May	29 November
13 May	23 May	28 November
2 June	12 June	27 November
17 May	27 May	2 December
9 May	19 May	1 December
29 May	8 June	30 November
14 May	24 May	29 November
5 May	15 May	27 November
25 May	4 June	3 December
10 May	20 May	2 December
30 May	9 June	1 December
21 May	31 May	29 November
13 May	23 May	28 November
26 May	5 June	27 November
18 May	28 May	3 December
9 May	19 May	1 December
29 May	8 June	30 November

Church Year (Advent to Advent)	Lectionary Year
1997/1998	C
1998/1999	A
1999/2000	B
2000/2001	C
2001/2002	A
2002/2003	B
2003/2004	C
2004/2005	A
2005/2006	B
2006/2007	C
2007/2008	A
2008/2009	B
2009/2010	C
2010/2011	A
2011/2012	B
2012/2013	C
2013/2014	A
2014/2015	B
2015/2016	C
2016/2017	A
2017/2018	B
2018/2019	C
2019/2020	A
2020/2021	B
2021/2022	C
2022/2023	A
2023/2024	B
2024/2025	C

January

1   **The Naming and Circumcision of Jesus**

2   Basil the Great and Gregory of Nazianzus, Bishops, Teachers of the
Faith, 379 and 389

2   *Seraphim, Monk of Sarov, Spiritual Guide, 1833*

2   *Vedanayagam Samuel Azariah, Bishop in South India, Evangelist, 1945*

6   **THE EPIPHANY**

10   *William Laud, Archbishop of Canterbury, 1645*

11   *Mary Slessor, Missionary in West Africa, 1915*

12   Aelred of Hexham, Abbot of Rievaulx, 1167

12   *Benedict Biscop, Abbot of Wearmouth, Scholar, 689*

13   Hilary, Bishop of Poitiers, Teacher of the Faith, 367

13   *Kentigern (Mungo), Missionary Bishop in Strathclyde and Cumbria, 603*

13   *George Fox, Founder of the Society of Friends (the Quakers), 1691*

17   Antony of Egypt, Hermit, Abbot, 356

17   *Charles Gore, Bishop, Founder of the Community of the Resurrection, 1932*

18-25   *Week of Prayer for Christian Unity*

19   Wulfstan, Bishop of Worcester, 1095

20   *Richard Rolle of Hampole, Spiritual Writer, 1349*

21   Agnes, Child-Martyr at Rome, 304

22   *Vincent of Saragossa, Deacon, first Martyr of Spain, 304*

24   Francis de Sales, Bishop of Geneva, Teacher of the Faith, 1622

25   **The Conversion of Paul**

26   Timothy and Titus, Companions of Paul

28   Thomas Aquinas, Priest, Philosopher, Teacher of the Faith, 1274

30   Charles, King and Martyr, 1649

31   *John Bosco, Priest, Founder of the Salesian Teaching Order, 1888*

February

1	*Brigid, Abbess of Kildare, c.525*
2	**THE PRESENTATION OF CHRIST IN THE TEMPLE** (CANDLEMAS)
3	Anskar, Archbishop of Hamburg, Missionary in Denmark and Sweden, 865
4	*Gilbert of Sempringham, Founder of the Gilbertine Order, 1189*
6	*The Martyrs of Japan, 1597*
10	*Scholastica, sister of Benedict, Abbess of Plombariola, c.543*
14	Cyril and Methodius, Missionaries to the Slavs, 869 and 885
14	*Valentine, Martyr at Rome, c.269*
15	*Sigfrid, Bishop, Apostle of Sweden, 1045*
15	*Thomas Bray, Priest, Founder of the SPCK and the SPG, 1730*
17	Janani Luwum, Archbishop of Uganda, Martyr, 1977
23	Polycarp, Bishop of Smyrna, Martyr, c.155
27	George Herbert, Priest, Poet, 1633

Alternative dates

Matthias may be celebrated on 24 February instead of 14 May.

March

1	David, Bishop of Menevia, Patron of Wales, c.601
2	Chad, Bishop of Lichfield, Missionary, 672
7	Perpetua, Felicity and their Companions, Martyrs at Carthage, 203
8	Edward King, Bishop of Lincoln, 1910
8	*Felix, Bishop, Apostle to the East Angles, 647*
8	*Geoffrey Studdert Kennedy, Priest, Poet, 1929*
17	Patrick, Bishop, Missionary, Patron of Ireland, c.460
18	*Cyril, Bishop of Jerusalem, Teacher of the Faith, 386*
19	**Joseph of Nazareth**
20	Cuthbert, Bishop of Lindisfarne, Missionary, 687
21	Thomas Cranmer, Archbishop of Canterbury, Reformation Martyr, 1556
24	*Walter Hilton of Thurgarton, Augustinian Canon, Mystic, 1396*
24	*Oscar Romero, Archbishop of San Salvador, Martyr, 1980*
25	**THE ANNUNCIATION OF OUR LORD TO THE BLESSED VIRGIN MARY**
26	*Harriet Monsell, Founder of the Community of St John the Baptist, Clewer, 1883*
31	*John Donne, Priest, Poet, 1631*

Alternative dates

Chad may be celebrated with Cedd on 26 October instead of 2 March.
Cuthbert may be celebrated on 4 September instead of 20 March.

April

May

1	**Philip and James, Apostles**
2	Athanasius, Bishop of Alexandria, Teacher of the Faith, 373
4	English Saints and Martyrs of the Reformation Era
8	Julian of Norwich, Spiritual Writer, c.1417
14	**Matthias the Apostle**
16	*Caroline Chisholm, Social Reformer, 1877*
19	Dunstan, Archbishop of Canterbury, Restorer of Monastic Life, 988
20	Alcuin of York, Deacon, Abbot of Tours, 804
21	*Helena, Protector of the Holy Places, 330*
23	*Petroc, Abbot of Padstow, 6th century*
24	John and Charles Wesley, Evangelists, Hymn Writers, 1791 and 1788
25	The Venerable Bede, Monk at Jarrow, Scholar, Historian, 735
25	*Aldhelm, Bishop of Sherborne, 709*
26	Augustine, first Archbishop of Canterbury, 605
26	*John Calvin, Reformer 1564*
26	*Philip Neri, Founder of the Oratorians, Spiritual Guide, 1595*
28	*Lanfranc, Prior of Le Bec, Archbishop of Canterbury, Scholar, 1089*
30	Josephine Butler, Social Reformer, 1906
30	*Joan of Arc, Visionary, 1431*
30	*Apolo Kivebulaya, Priest, Evangelist in Central Africa, 1933*
31	**The Visit of the Blessed Virgin Mary to Elizabeth**

Alternative dates

Matthias may be celebrated on 24 February instead of 14 May.
The Visit of the Blessed Virgin Mary to Elizabeth may be celebrated on 2 July instead of 31 May.

June

1	Justin, Martyr at Rome, c.165
3	*The Martyrs of Uganda, 1886 and 1978*
5	Boniface (Wynfrith) of Crediton, Bishop, Apostle of Germany, Martyr, 754
6	*Ini Kopuria, Founder of the Melanesian Brotherhood, 1945*
8	Thomas Ken, Bishop of Bath and Wells, Non-Juror, Hymn Writer, 1711
9	Columba, Abbot of Iona, Missionary, 597
9	*Ephrem of Syria, Deacon, Hymn Writer, Teacher of the Faith, 373*
11	**Barnabas the Apostle**
14	*Richard Baxter, Puritan Divine, 1691*
15	*Evelyn Underhill, Spiritual Writer, 1941*
16	Richard, Bishop of Chichester, 1253
16	*Joseph Butler, Bishop of Durham, Philosopher, 1752*
17	*Samuel and Henrietta Barnett, Social Reformers, 1913 and 1936*
18	*Bernard Mizeki, Apostle of the MaShona, Martyr, 1896*
19	*Sundar Singh of India, Sadhu (holy man), Evangelist, Teacher of the Faith, 1929*
22	Alban, first Martyr of Britain, c.250
23	Etheldreda, Abbess of Ely, c.678
24	**The Birth of John the Baptist**
27	*Cyril, Bishop of Alexandria, Teacher of the Faith, 444*
28	Irenæus, Bishop of Lyons, Teacher of the Faith, c.200
29	**Peter and Paul, Apostles**

Alternative dates

Peter the Apostle may be celebrated alone, without Paul, on 29 June.

July

1	*John and Henry Venn, Priests, Evangelical Divines, 1813 and 1873*
3	**Thomas the Apostle**
6	*Thomas More, Scholar, and John Fisher, Bishop of Rochester, Reformation Martyrs, 1535*
11	**Benedict of Nursia, Abbot of Monte Cassino, Father of Western Monasticism, c.550**
14	John Keble, Priest, Tractarian, Poet, 1866
15	Swithun, Bishop of Winchester, c.862
15	*Bonaventure, Friar, Bishop, Teacher of the Faith, 1274*
16	*Osmund, Bishop of Salisbury, 1099*
18	*Elizabeth Ferard, first Deaconess of the Church of England, Founder of the Community of St Andrew, 1883*
19	Gregory, Bishop of Nyssa, and his sister Macrina, Deaconess, Teachers of the Faith, c.394 and c.379
20	*Margaret of Antioch, Martyr, 4th Century*
20	*Bartolomé de las Casas, Apostle to the Indies, 1566*
22	**Mary Magdalene**
23	*Bridget of Sweden, Abbess of Vadstena, 1373*
25	**James the Apostle**
26	Anne and Joachim, Parents of the Blessed Virgin Mary
27	*Brooke Foss Westcott, Bishop of Durham, Teacher of the Faith, 1901*
29	Mary, Martha and Lazarus, Companions of our Lord
30	William Wilberforce, Social Reformer, 1833
31	*Ignatius of Loyola, Founder of the Society of Jesus, 1556*

Alternative dates

The Visit of the Blessed Virgin Mary to Elizabeth may be celebrated on 2 July instead of 31 May.
Thomas the Apostle may be celebrated on 21 December instead of 3 July.
Thomas Becket may be celebrated on 7 July instead of 29 December.

August

4	*Jean-Baptist Vianney, Curé d'Ars, Spiritual Guide, 1859*
5	Oswald, King of Northumbria, Martyr, 642
6	**The Transfiguration of our Lord**
7	*John Mason Neale, Priest, Hymn Writer, 1866*
8	Dominic, Priest, Founder of the Order of Preachers, 1221
9	Mary Sumner, Founder of the Mothers' Union, 1921
10	Laurence, Deacon at Rome, Martyr, 258
11	Clare of Assisi, Founder of the Minoresses (Poor Clares), 1253
11	*John Henry Newman, Priest, Tractarian, 1890*
13	Jeremy Taylor, Bishop of Down and Connor, Teacher of the Faith, 1667
13	*Florence Nightingale, Nurse, Social Reformer, 1910*
13	*Octavia Hill, Social Reformer, 1912*
14	*Maximilian Kolbe, Friar, Martyr, 1941*
15	**The Blessed Virgin Mary**
20	Bernard, Abbot of Clairvaux, Teacher of the Faith, 1153
20	*William and Catherine Booth, Founders of the Salvation Army, 1912 and 1890*
24	**Bartholomew the Apostle**
27	Monica, mother of Augustine of Hippo, 387
28	Augustine, Bishop of Hippo, Teacher of the Faith, 430
29	The Beheading of John the Baptist
30	John Bunyan, Spiritual Writer, 1688
31	Aidan, Bishop of Lindisfarne, Missionary, 651

Alternative dates

The Blessed Virgin Mary may be celebrated on 8 September instead of 15 August.

September

1	*Giles of Provence, Hermit, c.710*
2	*The Martyrs of Papua New Guinea, 1901 and 1942*
3	Gregory the Great, Bishop of Rome, Teacher of the Faith, 604
4	*Birinus, Bishop of Dorchester (Oxon), Apostle of Wessex, 650*
6	*Allen Gardiner, Missionary, founder of the South American Mission Society, 1851*
8	The Birth of the Blessed Virgin Mary
9	*Charles Fuge Lowder, Priest, 1880*
13	John Chrysostom, Bishop of Constantinople, Teacher of the Faith, 407
14	**Holy Cross Day**
15	Cyprian, Bishop of Carthage, Martyr, 258
16	Ninian, Bishop of Galloway, Apostle of the Picts, c.432
16	*Edward Bouverie Pusey, Priest, Tractarian, 1882*
17	Hildegard, Abbess of Bingen, Visionary, 1179
19	*Theodore of Tarsus, Archbishop of Canterbury, 690*
20	John Coleridge Patteson, First Bishop of Melanesia, and his Companions, Martyrs, 1871
21	**Matthew, Apostle and Evangelist**
25	Lancelot Andrewes, Bishop of Winchester, Spiritual Writer, 1626
25	*Sergei of Radonezh, Russian Monastic Reformer, Teacher of the Faith, 1392*
26	*Wilson Carlile, Founder of the Church Army, 1942*
27	Vincent de Paul, Founder of the Congregation of the Mission (Lazarists), 1660
29	**Michael and All Angels**
30	*Jerome, Translator of the Scriptures, Teacher of the Faith, 420*

Alternative dates

Cuthbert may be celebrated on 4 September instead of 20 March.

October

1	*Remigius, Bishop of Rheims, Apostle of the Franks, 533*
1	*Anthony Ashley Cooper, Earl of Shaftesbury, Social Reformer, 1885*
4	Francis of Assisi, Friar, Deacon, Founder of the Friars Minor, 1226
6	William Tyndale, Translator of the Scriptures, Reformation Martyr, 1536
9	*Denys, Bishop of Paris, and his Companions, Martyrs, c.250*
9	*Robert Grosseteste, Bishop of Lincoln, Philosopher, Scientist, 1253*
10	Paulinus, Bishop of York, Missionary, 644
10	*Thomas Traherne, Poet, Spiritual Writer, 1674*
11	*Ethelburga, Abbess of Barking, 675*
11	*James the Deacon, companion of Paulinus, 7th century*
12	Wilfrid of Ripon, Bishop, Missionary, 709
12	*Elizabeth Fry, Prison Reformer, 1845*
12	*Edith Cavell, Nurse, 1915*
13	Edward the Confessor, King of England, 1066
15	Teresa of Avila, Teacher of the Faith, 1582
16	*Nicholas Ridley, Bishop of London, and Hugh Latimer, Bishop of Worcester, Reformation Martyrs, 1555*
17	Ignatius, Bishop of Antioch, Martyr, c.107
18	**Luke the Evangelist**
19	Henry Martyn, Translator of the Scriptures, Missionary in India and Persia, 1812
25	*Crispin and Crispinian, Martyrs at Rome, c.287*
26	Alfred the Great, King of the West Saxons, Scholar, 899
26	*Cedd, Abbot of Lastingham, Bishop of the East Saxons, 664*
28	**Simon and Jude, Apostles**
29	James Hannington, Bishop of Eastern Equatorial Africa, Martyr in Uganda, 1885
31	*Martin Luther, Reformer, 1546*

Alternative dates

Chad may be celebrated with Cedd on 26 October instead of 2 March.

November

1	**ALL SAINTS' DAY**
2	Commemoration of the Faithful Departed (All Souls' Day)
3	Richard Hooker, Priest, Anglican Apologist, Teacher of the Faith, 1600
3	*Martin of Porres, Friar, 1639*
6	*Leonard, Hermit, 6th century*
6	*William Temple, Archbishop of Canterbury, Teacher of the Faith, 1944*
7	Willibrord of York, Bishop, Apostle of Frisia, 739
8	The Saints and Martyrs of England
9	*Margery Kempe, Mystic, c.1440*
10	Leo the Great, Bishop of Rome, Teacher of the Faith, 461
11	Martin, Bishop of Tours, c.397
13	Charles Simeon, Priest, Evangelical Divine, 1836
14	*Samuel Seabury, First Anglican Bishop in North America, 1796*
16	Margaret, Queen of Scotland, Philanthropist, Reformer of the Church, 1093
16	*Edmund Rich of Abingdon, Archbishop of Canterbury, 1240*
17	Hugh, Bishop of Lincoln, 1200
18	Elizabeth of Hungary, Princess of Thuringia, Philanthropist, 1231
19	Hilda, Abbess of Whitby, 680
19	*Mechtild, Béguine of Magdeburg, Mystic, 1280*
20	Edmund, King of the East Angles, Martyr, 870
20	*Priscilla Lydia Sellon, a Restorer of the Religious Life in the Church of England, 1876*
22	*Cecilia, Martyr at Rome, c.230*
23	Clement, Bishop of Rome, Martyr, c.100
25	*Catherine of Alexandria, Martyr, 4th century*
25	*Isaac Watts, Hymn Writer, 1748*
29	*Day of Intercession and Thanksgiving for the Missionary Work of the Church*
30	**Andrew the Apostle**

December

1	*Charles de Foucauld, Hermit in the Sahara, 1916*
3	*Francis Xavier, Missionary, Apostle of the Indies, 1552*
4	*John of Damascus, Monk, Teacher of the Faith, c.749*
4	*Nicholas Ferrar, Deacon, Founder of the Little Gidding Community, 1637*
6	Nicholas, Bishop of Myra, c.326
7	Ambrose, Bishop of Milan, Teacher of the Faith, 397
8	The Conception of the Blessed Virgin Mary
13	Lucy, Martyr at Syracuse, 304
13	*Samuel Johnson, Moralist, 1784*
14	John of the Cross, Poet, Teacher of the Faith, 1591
17	*O Sapientia*
17	*Eglantine Jebb, Social Reformer, Founder of 'Save The Children', 1928*
24	Christmas Eve
25	**CHRISTMAS DAY**
26	**Stephen, Deacon, First Martyr**
27	**John, Apostle and Evangelist**
28	**The Holy Innocents**
29	Thomas Becket, Archbishop of Canterbury, Martyr, 1170
31	*John Wyclif, Reformer, 1384*

Alternative dates

Thomas the Apostle may be celebrated on 21 December instead of 3 July.
Thomas Becket may be celebrated on 7 July instead of 29 December.

THE
LECTIONARY

1 The references in the following tables, including those to the psalms, are to the *New Revised Standard Version* of the Bible. When other versions are used, such adaptations may be made as are necessary.

The references in the following tables, including those to the psalms, state book, chapter and verse in that order. Where optional additional verses or psalms are set, the references are placed in square parentheses [. . .]. A simple choice between two alternative readings is indicated by an italicized *or*, placed between references. Longer psalms, which are starred thus*, have optional shorter alternatives given in the tables on pages 95 and 96.

2 When a reading begins with a personal pronoun, the reader may substitute the appropriate noun.

3 In these tables, verses are stated inclusively. The letter *a* after the number of a verse signifies the first part of that verse; the letter *b* the second part.

4 In a compact cycle of readings such as these, some passages have necessarily been abbreviated. When opportunity allows, the passages may be read in full. Verses in brackets may be included or omitted, as desired.

5 When there are only two readings at the Principal Service and that service is Holy Communion, the second reading is always the Gospel reading.

If there are only two readings at the Principal Service on Ascension Day, Pentecost, the Conversion of Paul or the festivals of Matthias, Barnabas, James and Stephen, the reading from the Acts of the Apostles must always be used.

In the choice of readings other than the Gospel reading, the minister should ensure that, in any year, a balance is maintained between readings from the Old and New Testaments and that, where a particular biblical book is appointed to be read over several weeks, the choice ensures that this continuity of one book is not lost.

When the Principal Service lectionary is used at a service other than Holy Communion, the Gospel reading need not always be chosen.

6 During the period from the First Sunday of Advent to the Presentation of Christ in the Temple, during the period from Ash Wednesday to Trinity Sunday, and on All Saints' Day, the readings shall come from an authorized lectionary. During Ordinary Time (i.e. between the Presentation and Ash Wednesday and between Trinity Sunday and Advent Sunday), authorized lectionary provision remains the norm but, after due consultation with the Parochial Church Council, the minister may, from time to time, depart from the lectionary provision for pastoral reasons or preaching or teaching purposes.

7 Three sets of psalms and readings are provided for each Sunday. The Principal Service Lectionary (which is drawn from the Revised Common Lectionary) is intended for use at the principal service of the day (whether this service is Holy Communion or some other authorized form). In most church communities, this is likely to be the mid-morning service, but the minister is free to decide which service time normally constitutes the principal service of the day.

The Second Service Lectionary is intended for a second main service. In many churches, this lectionary will be the appropriate provision for a Sunday afternoon or evening service. A Gospel reading is always provided so that this lectionary can, if necessary, be used at Holy Communion.

The Third Service Lectionary, with shorter readings, is intended where a third set of psalms and readings is needed and is most appropriate for use at an office.

8 Where a festival is celebrated on a Sunday, the Morning Prayer provision is used at the service using the Second Service Lectionary, and the Evening Prayer provision is used at the service using the Third Service Lectionary.

9 On the Sundays between the Presentation of Christ in the Temple and the Second Sunday before Lent, and again on the Sundays after Trinity, the readings and collects follow independent courses. The collects and post communion prayers are attached to the Sunday title (The Fifth/Fourth/Third Sunday before Lent, The First/Second/Third Sunday after Trinity, etc.), but the sets of proper readings (Propers 4, 5, 6) belong to particular calendar dates (i.e. the Sunday between two dates).

10 On the Sundays after Trinity, the Principal Service Lectionary provides alternative Old Testament readings and psalms. Those under the heading 'Continuous' allow the Old Testament reading and its complementary psalm to stand independently of the other readings. Those under the heading 'Related' relate the Old Testament reading and the psalm to the Gospel reading. It is unhelpful to move from week to week from one column to another. One column should be followed for the whole sequence of Sundays after Trinity.

The First Sunday of Advent

YEAR A	YEAR B	YEAR C
Principal Service		
Isaiah 2.1-5	Isaiah 64.1-9	Jeremiah 33.14-16
Psalm 122	Psalm 80.1-7,17-19*	Psalm 25.1-10
Romans 13.11-14	1 Corinthians 1.3-9	1 Thessalonians 3.9-13
Matthew 24.36-44	Mark 13.24-37	Luke 21.25-36
Second Service		
Psalm 9*	Psalm 25*	Psalm 9*
Isaiah 52.1-12	Isaiah 1.1-20	Joel 3.9-21
Matthew 24.15-28	Matthew 21.1-13	Revelation 14.13 – 15.4
		If the Second Service is a Eucharist, the following is read as a Gospel:
		John 3.1-17
Third Service		
Psalm 44	Psalm 44	Psalm 44
Micah 4.1-7	Isaiah 2.1-5	Isaiah 51.4-11
1 Thessalonians 5.1-11	Luke 12.35-48	Romans 13.11-14

The Second Sunday of Advent

YEAR A	YEAR B	YEAR C
Principal Service		
Isaiah 11.1-10	Isaiah 40.1-11	Baruch 5.1-9 or
Psalm 72.1-7,18-19*	Psalm 85.1-2,8-13*	Malachi 3.1-4
Romans 15.4-13	2 Peter 3.8-15a	*Canticle:* Benedictus
Matthew 3.1-12	Mark 1.1-8	Philippians 1.3-11
		Luke 3.1-6
Second Service		
Psalms 11 [28]	Psalm 40*	Psalms 75 [76]
1 Kings 18.17-39	1 Kings 22.1-28	Isaiah 40.1-11
John 1.19-28	Romans 15.4-13	Luke 1.1-25
	If the Second Service is a Eucharist, the following is read as a Gospel:	
	Matthew 11.2-11	
Third Service		
Psalm 80	Psalm 80	Psalm 80
Amos 7	Baruch 5.1-9 or	Isaiah 64.1-7
Luke 1.5-20	Zephaniah 3.14-20	Matthew 11.2-11
	Luke 1.5-20	

The Third Sunday of Advent

YEAR A	YEAR B	YEAR C
Principal Service		

Isaiah 35.1-10
Psalm 146.5-10 *or*
  Canticle: Magnificat
James 5.7-10
Matthew 11.2-11
	Isaiah 61.1-4,8-11
	Psalm 126 *or*
	  Canticle: Magnificat
	1 Thessalonians 5.16-24
	John 1.6-8,19-28
		Zephaniah 3.14-20
		Canticle: Isaiah 12.2-6*
		Philippians 4.4-7
		Luke 3.7-18

Second Service		
Psalms 12 [14] Isaiah 5.8-30 Acts 13.13-41 If the Second Service is a Eucharist, the following is read as a Gospel: John 5.31-40	Psalm 68.1-20* Malachi 3.1-4; 4 Philippians 4.4-7 If the Second Service is a Eucharist, the following is read as a Gospel: Matthew 14.1-12	Psalms 50.1-6 [62] Isaiah 35 Luke 1.57-66[67-80]
Third Service		
Psalm 68.1-20 Zephaniah 3.14-20 Philippians 4.4-7	Psalms 50.1-6, 62 Isaiah 12 Luke 1.57-66	Psalms 12, 14 Isaiah 25.1-9 1 Corinthians 4.1-5

The Fourth Sunday of Advent

YEAR A	YEAR B	YEAR C
Principal Service		

Isaiah 7.10-16
Psalm 80.1-7,17-19*
Romans 1.1-7
Matthew 1.18-25
	2 Samuel 7.1-11,16
	Canticle: Magnificat *or*
	  Psalm 89.1-4,19-26*
	Romans 16.25-27
	Luke 1.26-38
		Micah 5.2-5a
		Canticle: Magnificat *or*
		  Psalm 80.1-7
		Hebrews 10.5-10
		Luke 1.39-45[46-55]

Second Service		
Psalms 113 [126] 1 Samuel 1.1-20 Revelation 22.6-21 If the Second Service is a Eucharist, the following is read as a Gospel: Luke 1.39-45	Psalms 113 [131] Zechariah 2.10-13 Luke 1.39-55	Psalms 123 [131] Isaiah 10.33 – 11.10 Matthew 1.18-25
Third Service		
Psalm 144 Micah 5.2-5a Luke 1.26-38	Psalm 144 Isaiah 7.10-16 Romans 1.1-7	Psalm 144 Isaiah 32.1-8 Revelation 22.6-21

Christmas Eve

Morning Eucharist Years A, B, C
2 Samuel 7.1-5,8-11,16
Psalm 89.2,21-27
Acts 13.16-26
Luke 1.67-79

Evening Prayer Years A, B, C
Psalm 85
Zechariah 2
Revelation 1.1-8

Christmas Day

25 December

Principal Service Years A, B, C		
Any of the following sets of readings may be used on the evening of Christmas Eve and on Christmas Day. Set III should be used at some service during the celebration.		
I	II	III
Isaiah 9.2-7	Isaiah 62.6-12	Isaiah 52.7-10
Psalm 96	Psalm 97	Psalm 98
Titus 2.11-14	Titus 3.4-7	Hebrews 1.1-4[5-12]
Luke 2.1-14[15-20]	Luke 2.[1-7]8-20	John 1.1-14

Second Service Years A, B, C
Psalm 8
Isaiah 65.17-25
Philippians 2.5-11
or Luke 2.1-20
if it has not been used at the Principal Service of the day

Third Service Years A, B, C
Psalm 110
Isaiah 62.1-5
Matthew 1.18-25

The First Sunday of Christmas

YEAR A	YEAR B	YEAR C
Principal Service		
Isaiah 63.7-9 Psalm 148* Hebrews 2.10-18 Matthew 2.13-23	Isaiah 61.10 – 62.3 Psalm 148* Galatians 4.4-7 Luke 2.15-21	1 Samuel 2.18-20,26 Psalm 148* Colossians 3.12-17 Luke 2.41-52
Second Service		
Psalm 132 Isaiah 49.7-13 Philippians 2.1-11 If the Second Service is a Eucharist, the following is read as a Gospel: Luke 2.41-52	Psalm 132 Isaiah 35.1-10 Colossians 1.9-20 or Luke 2.41-52	Psalm 132 Isaiah 61 Galatians 3.27 – 4.7 If the Second Service is a Eucharist, the following is read as a Gospel: Luke 2.15-21
Third Service		
Psalm 105.1-9 Isaiah 35.1-6 Galatians 3.23-25	Psalm 105.1-9 Isaiah 63.7-9 Ephesians 3.5-12	Psalm 105.1-11 Isaiah 41.21 – 42.1 1 John 1.1-7

The Second Sunday of Christmas

YEAR A	YEAR B	YEAR C
Principal Service (Readings for Years A, B, C are the same)		
Jeremiah 31.7-14 Psalm 147.12-20 Ephesians 1.3-14 John 1.[1-9]10-18 or Ecclesiasticus 24.1-12 Canticle: Wisdom of Solomon 10.15-21 Ephesians 1.3-14 John 1.[1-9]10-18	Jeremiah 31.7-14 Psalm 147.12-20 Ephesians 1.3-14 John 1.[1-9]10-18 or Ecclesiasticus 24.1-12 Canticle: Wisdom of Solomon 10.15-21 Ephesians 1.3-14 John 1.[1-9]10-18	Jeremiah 31.7-14 Psalm 147.12-20 Ephesians 1.3-14 John 1.[1-9]10-18 or Ecclesiasticus 24.1-12 Canticle: Wisdom of Solomon 10.15-21 Ephesians 1.3-14 John 1.[1-9]10-18
Second Service		
Psalm 135* Isaiah 41.21 – 42.4 Colossians 1.1-14 If the Second Service is a Eucharist, the following is read as a Gospel: Matthew 2.13-23	Psalm 135* Isaiah 46.3-13 Romans 12.1-8 If the Second Service is a Eucharist, the following is read as a Gospel: Matthew 2.13-23	Psalm 135 1 Samuel 1.20-28 1 John 4.7-16 If the Second Service is a Eucharist, the following is read as a Gospel: Matthew 2.13-23
Third Service		
Psalm 87 Jeremiah 31.15-17 2 Corinthians 1.3-12	Psalm 87 Zechariah 8.1-8 Luke 2.41-52	Psalm 87 Isaiah 12 2 Thessalonians 2.1-8

The Epiphany

6 January

Evening Prayer on the Eve Years A, B, C
Psalms 96, 97
Isaiah 49.1-13
John 4.7-26

Principal Service Years A, B, C
Isaiah 60.1-6
Psalm 72.[1-9]10-15
Ephesians 3.1-12
Matthew 2.1-12

Second Service Years A, B, C
Psalms 98, 100
Baruch 4.36 – 5.9 *or*
Isaiah 60.1-9
John 2.1-11

Third Service Years A, B, C
Psalms 113, 132
Jeremiah 31.7-14
John 1.29-34

The Baptism of Christ
The First Sunday of Epiphany

Evening Prayer on the Eve (if required)
Psalm 36 Isaiah 61 Titus 2.11-14;3.4-7

YEAR A	YEAR B	YEAR C
Principal Service		
Isaiah 42.1-9 Psalm 29 Acts 10.34-43 Matthew 3.13-17	Genesis 1.1-5 Psalm 29 Acts 19.1-7 Mark 1.4-11	Isaiah 43.1-7 Psalm 29 Acts 8.14-17 Luke 3.15-17,21-22
Second Service		
Psalms 46, 47 Joshua 3.1-8,14-17 Hebrews 1.1-12 If the Second Service is a Eucharist, the following is read as a Gospel: Luke 3.15-22	Psalms 46 [47] Isaiah 42.1-9 Ephesians 2.1-10 If the Second Service is a Eucharist, the following is read as a Gospel: Matthew 3.13-17	Psalms 46, 47 Isaiah 55.1-11 Romans 6.1-11 If the Second Service is a Eucharist, the following is read as a Gospel: Mark 1.4-11
Third Service		
Psalm 89.20-29 Exodus 14.15-22 1 John 5.6-9	Psalm 89.20-29 1 Samuel 16.1-3,13 John 1.29-34	Psalm 89.19-29 Isaiah 42.1-9 Acts 19.1-7

The Second Sunday of Epiphany

YEAR A	YEAR B	YEAR C
Principal Service		
Isaiah 49.1-7 Psalm 40.1-11 1 Corinthians 1.1-9 John 1.29-42	1 Samuel 3.1-10[11-20] Psalm 139.1-6,13-18* Revelation 5.1-10 John 1.43-51	Isaiah 62.1-5 Psalm 36.5-10 1 Corinthians 12.1-11 John 2.1-11
Second Service		
Psalm 96 Ezekiel 2.1 – 3.4 Galatians 1.11-24 If the Second Service is a Eucharist, the following is read as a Gospel: John 1.43-51	Psalm 96 Isaiah 60.9-22 Hebrews 6.17 – 7.10 If the Second Service is a Eucharist, the following is read as a Gospel: Matthew 8.5-13	Psalm 96 1 Samuel 3.1-20 Ephesians 4.1-16 If the Second Service is a Eucharist, the following is read as a Gospel: John 1.29-42
Third Service		
Psalm 145.1-12 Jeremiah 1.4-10 Mark 1.14-20	Psalm 145.1-12 Isaiah 62.1-5 1 Corinthians 6.11-20	Psalm 145.1-13 Isaiah 49.1-7 Acts 16.11-15

The Third Sunday of Epiphany

YEAR A	YEAR B	YEAR C
Principal Service		
Isaiah 9.1-4 Psalm 27.1,4-9* 1 Corinthians 1.10-18 Matthew 4.12-23	Genesis 14.17-20 Psalm 128 Revelation 19.6-10 John 2.1-11	Nehemiah 8.1-3,5-6, 8-10 Psalm 19* 1 Corinthians 12.12- 31a Luke 4.14-21
Second Service		
Psalm 33* Ecclesiastes 3.1-11 1 Peter 1.3-12 If the Second Service is a Eucharist, the following is read as a Gospel: Luke 4.14-21	Psalm 33* Jeremiah 3.21 – 4.2 Titus 2.1-8,11-14 If the Second Service is a Eucharist, the following is read as a Gospel: Matthew 4.12-23	Psalm 33 Numbers 9.15-23 1 Corinthians 7.17-24 If the Second Service is a Eucharist, the following is read as a Gospel: Mark 1.21-28
Third Service		
Psalm 113 Amos 3.1-8 1 John 1.1-4	Psalm 113 Jonah 3.1-5,10 John 3.16-21	Psalm 113 Deuteronomy 30.11- 15 3 John 1,5-8

The Fourth Sunday of Epiphany

YEAR A	YEAR B	YEAR C
Principal Service		
1 Kings 17.8-16 Psalm 36.5-10 1 Corinthians 1.18-31 John 2.1-11	Deuteronomy 18.15- 20 Psalm 111 Revelation 12.1-5a Mark 1.21-28	Ezekiel 43.27 – 44.4 Psalm 48 1 Corinthians 13.1-13 Luke 2.22-40
Second Service		
Psalm 34* Genesis 28.10-22 Philemon 1-16 If the Second Service is a Eucharist, the following is read as a Gospel: Mark 1.21-28	Psalm 34* 1 Samuel 3.1-20 1 Corinthians 14.12-20 If the Second Service is a Eucharist, the following is read as a Gospel: Matthew 13.10-17	Psalm 34 1 Chronicles 29.6-19 Acts 7.44-50 If the Second Service is a Eucharist, the following is read as a Gospel: John 4.19-29a
Third Service		
Psalm 71.1-6,15-17 Haggai 2.1-9 1 Corinthians 3.10-17	Psalm 71.1-6,15-17 Jeremiah 1.4-10 Mark 1.40-45	Psalm 71.1-6,15-17 Micah 6.1-8 1 Corinthians 6.12-20

The Presentation of Christ in the Temple
Candlemas

2 February

Ordinary Time

Proper 1

Sunday between 3 and 9 February inclusive (if earlier than the Second Sunday before Lent)

YEAR A	YEAR B	YEAR C
Principal Service		
Isaiah 58.1-9a[b-12] Psalm 112.1-9[10] 1 Corinthians 2.1-12 [13-16] Matthew 5.13-20	Isaiah 40.21-31 Psalm 147.1-11,20c* 1 Corinthians 9.16-23 Mark 1.29-39	Isaiah 6.1-8[9-13] Psalm 138 1 Corinthians 15.1-11 Luke 5.1-11
Second Service		
Psalms [1, 3] 4 Amos 2.4-16 Ephesians 4.17-32 If the Second Service is a Eucharist, the following is read as a Gospel: Mark 1.29-39	Psalm 5 Numbers 13.1-2,27-33 Philippians 2.12-28 If the Second Service is a Eucharist, the following is read as a Gospel: Luke 5.1-11	Psalms [1] 2 Wisdom 6.1-21 *or* Hosea 1 Colossians 3.1-22 If the Second Service is a Eucharist, the following is read as a Gospel: Matthew 5.13-20
Third Service		
Psalms 5, 6 Jeremiah 26.1-16 Acts 3.1-10	Psalms 2, 3 Jeremiah 26.1-16 Acts 3.1-10	Psalms 3, 4 Jeremiah 26.1-16 Acts 3.1-10

Proper 2

Sunday between 10 and 16 February inclusive (if earlier than the Second Sunday before Lent)

YEAR A	YEAR B	YEAR C
Principal Service		
Deuteronomy 30.15-20 *or* Ecclesiasticus 15.15-20 Psalm 119.1-8 1 Corinthians 3.1-9 Matthew 5.21-37	2 Kings 5.1-14 Psalm 30 1 Corinthians 9.24-27 Mark 1.40-45	Jeremiah 17.5-10 Psalm 1 1 Corinthians 15.12-20 Luke 6.17-26
Second Service		
Psalms [7] 13 Amos 3.1-8 Ephesians 5.1-17 If the Second Service is a Eucharist, the following is read as a Gospel: Mark 1.40-45	Psalm 6 Numbers 20.2-13 Philippians 3.7-21 If the Second Service is a Eucharist, the following is read as a Gospel: Luke 6.17-26	Psalms [5] 6 Wisdom 11.21 – 12.11 *or* Hosea 10.1-8,12 Galatians 4.8-20 If the Second Service is a Eucharist, the following is read as a Gospel: Matthew 5.21-37
Third Service		
Psalm 10 Jeremiah 30.1-3,10-22 Acts 6	Psalm 7 Jeremiah 30.1-3,10-22 Acts 6	Psalm 7 Jeremiah 30.1-3,10-22 Acts 6

Proper 3

Sunday between 17 and 23 February inclusive (if earlier than the Second Sunday before Lent)

YEAR A	YEAR B	YEAR C
Principal Service		
Leviticus 19.1-2,9-18 Psalm 119.33-40 1 Corinthians 3.10-11, 16-23 Matthew 5.38-48	Isaiah 43.18-25 Psalm 41 2 Corinthians 1.18-22 Mark 2.1-12	Genesis 45.3-11,15 Psalm 37.1-11,39-40* 1 Corinthians 15.35-38, 42-50 Luke 6.27-38
Second Service		
Psalm 18.1-19 *or* 18.20-29 Amos 9.5-15 Ephesians 6.1-20 If the Second Service is a Eucharist, the following is read as a Gospel: Mark 2.1-12	Psalm 10 Numbers 22.21 – 23.12 Philippians 4.10-20 If the Second Service is a Eucharist, the following is read as a Gospel: Luke 6.27-38	Psalms [11] 13 Hosea 14 Galatians 5.2-10 If the Second Service is a Eucharist, the following is read as a Gospel: Matthew 6.1-8
Third Service		
Psalms 21, 23 Jeremiah 33.1-11 Acts 8.4-25	Psalm 9 Jeremiah 33.1-11 Acts 8.4-25	Psalm 10 Jeremiah 33.1-11 Acts 8.4-25

The Second Sunday Before Lent

YEAR A	YEAR B	YEAR C
Principal Service		
Genesis 1.1 – 2.3 Psalm 136 *or* Psalm 136.1-9,23-26 Romans 8.18-25 Matthew 6.25-34	Proverbs 8.1,22-31 Psalm 104.24-35 Colossians 1.15-20 John 1.1-14	Genesis 2.4b-9,15-25 Psalm 65 Revelation 4 Luke 8.22-25
Second Service		
Psalm 148 Proverbs 8.1,22-31 Revelation 4 If the Second Service is a Eucharist, the following is read as a Gospel: Luke 12.16-31	Psalm 65 Genesis 2.4b-25 Luke 8.22-35	Psalm 147* Genesis 1.1 – 2.3 Matthew 6.25-34
Third Service		
Psalms 100, 150 Job 38.1-21 Colossians 1.15-20	Psalms 29, 67 Deuteronomy 8.1-10 Matthew 6.25-34	Psalm 104.1-25 Job 28.1-11 Acts 14.8-17

The Sunday Next Before Lent

YEAR A	YEAR B	YEAR C
Principal Service		

Exodus 24.12-18
Psalm 2
  or Psalm 99
2 Peter 1.16-21
Matthew 17.1-9
	2 Kings 2.1-12
	Psalm 50.1-6
	2 Corinthians 4.3-6
	Mark 9.2-9
		Exodus 34.29-35
		Psalm 99
		2 Corinthians 3.12 –
		  4.2
		Luke 9.28-36[37-43]

Second Service		
Psalm 84 Ecclesiasticus 48.1-10 or 2 Kings 2.1-12 Matthew 17.9-23 (*or* 1-23)	Psalms 2 [99] 1 Kings 19.1-16 2 Peter 1.16-21 If the Second Service is a Eucharist, the following is read as a Gospel: Mark 9.[2-8]9-13	Psalm 89.1-18* Exodus 3.1-6 John 12.27-36a
Third Service		
Psalm 72 Exodus 34.29-35 2 Corinthians 4.3-6	Psalms 27, 150 Exodus 24.12-18 2 Corinthians 3.12-18	Psalm 2 Exodus 33.17-23 1 John 3.1-3

Ash Wednesday

The First Sunday of Lent

The Second Sunday of Lent

YEAR A	YEAR B	YEAR C
Principal Service		
Genesis 12.1-4a	Genesis 17.1-7,15-16	Genesis 15.1-12,17-18
Psalm 121	Psalm 22.23-31	Psalm 27
Romans 4.1-5,13-17	Romans 4.13-25	Philippians 3.17 – 4.1
John 3.1-17	Mark 8.31-38	Luke 13.31-35
Second Service		
Psalm 135*	Psalm 135*	Psalm 135
Numbers 21.4-9	Genesis 12.1-9	Jeremiah 22.1-9,13-17
Luke 14.27-33	Hebrews 11.1-3,8-16	Luke 14.27-33
Third Service		
Psalm 74	Psalm 105.1-6,37-45	Psalm 119.161-176
Jeremiah 22.1-9	Isaiah 51.1-11	Genesis 17.1-7,15-16
Matthew 8.1-13	Galatians 3.1-9,23-29	Romans 11.13-24

The Third Sunday of Lent

YEAR A	YEAR B	YEAR C
Principal Service		
Exodus 17.1-7	Exodus 20.1-17	Isaiah 55.1-9
Psalm 95	Psalm 19*	Psalm 63.1-8
Romans 5.1-11	1 Corinthians 1.18-25	1 Corinthians 10.1-13
John 4.5-42	John 2.13-22	Luke 13.1-9
Second Service		
Psalm 40	Psalms 11, 12	Psalms 12, 13
Joshua 1.1-9	Exodus 5.1 – 6.1	Genesis 28.10-19a
Ephesians 6.10-20	Philippians 3.4b-14 *or*	John 1.35-51
If the Second Service is a Eucharist, the following is read as a Gospel:	Matthew 10.16-22	
John 2.13-22		
Third Service		
Psalm 46	Psalm 18.1-24	Psalms 26, 28
Amos 7.10-17	Jeremiah 38	Deuteronomy 6.4-9
2 Corinthians 1.1-11	Philippians 1.1-26	John 17.1a,11b-19

The Fourth Sunday of Lent

YEAR A	YEAR B	YEAR C
Principal Service		
1 Samuel 16.1-13 Psalm 23 Ephesians 5.8-14 John 9.1-41	Numbers 21.4-9 Psalm 107.1-3,17-22* Ephesians 2.1-10 John 3.14-21	Joshua 5.9-12 Psalm 32 2 Corinthians 5.16-21 Luke 15.1-3,11b-32
Second Service		
Psalm 31.1-16 *or* 31.1-8 Micah 7 *or* Prayer of Manasseh James 5 If the Second Service is a Eucharist, the following is read as a Gospel: John 3.14-21	Psalms 13, 14 Exodus 6.2-13 Romans 5.1-11 If the Second Service is a Eucharist, the following is read as a Gospel: John 12.1-8	Psalm 30 Prayer of Manasseh *or* Isaiah 40.27 – 41.13 2 Timothy 4.1-18 If the Second Service is a Eucharist, the following is read as a Gospel: John 11.17-44

If the Principal Service readings have been displaced by Mothering Sunday provisions, they may be used at the Second Service.

Third Service		
Psalm 19 Isaiah 43.1-7 Ephesians 2.8-14	Psalm 27 1 Samuel 16.1-13 John 9.1-25	Psalms 84, 85 Genesis 37.3-4,12-36 1 Peter 2.16-25

Mothering Sunday

Principal Service Years A, B, C
Exodus 2.1-10 *or* 1 Samuel 1.20-28 Psalm 34.11-20 *or* Psalm 127.1-4 2 Corinthians 1.3-7 *or* Colossians 3.12-17 Luke 2.33-35 *or* John 19.25-27

The Fifth Sunday of Lent
Passiontide begins

YEAR A	YEAR B	YEAR C
Principal Service		
Ezekiel 37.1-14	Jeremiah 31.31-34	Isaiah 43.16-21
Psalm 130	Psalm 51.1-12 *or*	Psalm 126
Romans 8.6-11	Psalm 119.9-16	Philippians 3.4b-14
John 11.1-45	Hebrews 5.5-10	John 12.1-8
	John 12.20-33	
Second Service		
Psalm 30	Psalm 34*	Psalm 35*
Lamentations 3.19-33	Exodus 7.8-24	2 Chronicles 35.1-6,
Matthew 20.17-34	Romans 5.12-21	10-16
	If the Second Service is a Eucharist, the following is read as a Gospel:	Luke 22.1-13
	Luke 22.1-13	
Third Service		
Psalm 86	Psalm 107.1-22	Psalms 111, 112
Jeremiah 31.27-37	Exodus 24.3-8	Isaiah 35.1-10
John 12.20-33	Hebrews 12.18-29	Romans 7.21 – 8.4

Palm Sunday

YEAR A	YEAR B	YEAR C
Principal Service		
LITURGY OF THE PALMS:	LITURGY OF THE PALMS:	LITURGY OF THE PALMS:
Matthew 21.1-11	Mark 11.1-11 *or*	Luke 19.28-40
Psalm 118.1-2,19-29*	John 12.12-16	Psalm 118.1-2,19-29*
	Psalm 118.1-2,19-24*	
LITURGY OF THE PASSION:	LITURGY OF THE PASSION:	LITURGY OF THE PASSION:
Isaiah 50.4-9a	Isaiah 50.4-9a	Isaiah 50.4-9a
Psalm 31.9-16*	Psalm 31.9-16*	Psalm 31.9-16*
Philippians 2.5-11	Philippians 2.5-11	Philippians 2.5-11
Matthew 26.14 –	Mark 14.1 – 15.47 *or*	Luke 22.14 – 23.56 *or*
27.66 *or*	Mark 15.1-39[40-47]	Luke 23.1-49
Matthew 27.11-54		
Second Service		
Psalm 80	Psalm 69.1-18	Psalm 69.1-18
Isaiah 5.1-7	Isaiah 5.1-7	Isaiah 5.1-7
Matthew 21.33-46	Mark 12.1-12	Luke 20.9-19
Third Service		
Psalms 61, 62	Psalms 61, 62	Psalms 61, 62
Zechariah 9.9-12	Zechariah 9.9-12	Zechariah 9.9-12
Luke 16.19-31	1 Corinthians 2.1-12	1 Corinthians 2.1-12

Monday of Holy Week

Principal Service Years A, B, C

Isaiah 42.1-9
Psalm 36.5-11
Hebrews 9.11-15
John 12.1-11

Second Service Years A, B, C

Psalm 41
Lamentations 1.1-12a
Luke 22.1-23

Third Service Years A, B, C

Psalm 25
Lamentations 2.8-19
Colossians 1.18-23

Tuesday of Holy Week

Principal Service Years A, B, C

Isaiah 49.1-7
Psalm 71.1-14*
1 Corinthians 1.18-31
John 12.20-36

Second Service Years A, B, C

Psalm 27
Lamentations 3.1-18
Luke 22.24-53 (or
  39-53)

Third Service Years A, B, C

Psalm 55.12-22
Lamentations 3.40-51
Galatians 6.11-18

Wednesday of Holy Week

Principal Service Years A, B, C
Isaiah 50.4-9a Psalm 70 Hebrews 12.1-3 John 13.21-32
Second Service Years A, B, C

Psalm 102*
Wisdom 1.16 – 2.1;
  2.12-22 *or*
  Jeremiah 11.18-20
Luke 22.54-71

Third Service Years A, B, C
Psalm 88 Isaiah 63.1-9 Revelation 14.18 –   15.4

Maundy Thursday

Principal Service Years A, B, C
Exodus 12.1-4[5-10]   11-14 Psalm 116.1-2,12-19* 1 Corinthians 11.23-26 John 13.1-17,31b-35
Second Service Years A, B, C
Psalm 39 Leviticus 16.2-24 Luke 23.1-25
Third Service Years A, B, C
Psalms 42, 43 Exodus 11 Ephesians 2.11-18

Good Friday

Principal Service Years A, B, C

Isaiah 52.13 – 53.12
Psalm 22*
Hebrews 10.16-25 or
  Hebrews 4.14-16;
  5.7-9
John 18.1 – 19.42

Second Service Years A, B, C

Psalms 130, 143
Genesis 22.1-18
A part of John 18-19
if not used at the Principal Service
especially in the evening,
John 19.38-42 or
  Colossians 1.18-23

Third Service Years A, B, C

Psalm 69
Lamentations 5.15-22
A part of John 18-19
if not read at the Principal Service
  or Hebrews 10.1-10

Easter Eve

Principal Service Years A, B, C

*These readings are for
use at services other
than the Easter Vigil.*
Job 14.1-14 or
  Lamentations 3.1-9,
  19-24
Psalm 31.1-4,15-16*
1 Peter 4.1-8
Matthew 27.57-66 or
  John 19.38-42

Second Service Years A, B, C

Psalm 142
Hosea 6.1-6
John 2.18-22

Third Service Years A, B, C

Psalm 116
Job 19.21-27
1 John 5.5-12

Easter Vigil

YEAR A

A minimum of three Old Testament readings should be chosen. The reading from Exodus 14 should always be used.

Genesis 1.1 – 2.4a	Psalm 136.1-9,23-26
Genesis 7.1-5,11-18; 8.6-18; 9.8-13	Psalm 46
Genesis 22.1-18	Psalm 16
Exodus 14.10-31; 15.20-21	*Canticle:* **Exodus 15.1b-13,17-18**
Isaiah 55.1-11	*Canticle:* Isaiah 12.2-6
Baruch 3.9-15,32 – 4.4	
or Proverbs 8.1-8,19-21; 9.4b-6	Psalm 19
Ezekiel 36.24-28	Psalms 42, 43
Ezekiel 37.1-14	Psalm 143
Zephaniah 3.14-20	Psalm 98
Romans 6.3-11	**Psalm 114**
Matthew 28.1-10	

YEAR B

A minimum of three Old Testament readings should be chosen. The reading from Exodus 14 should always be used.

Genesis 1.1 – 2.4a	Psalm 136.1-9,23-26
Genesis 7.1-5,11-18; 8.6-18; 9.8-13	Psalm 46
Genesis 22.1-18	Psalm 16
Exodus 14.10-31; 15.20-21	*Canticle:* **Exodus 15.1b-13,17-18**
Isaiah 55.1-11	*Canticle:* Isaiah 12.2-6
Baruch 3.9-15,32 – 4.4	
or Proverbs 8.1-8,19-21; 9.4b-6	Psalm 19
Ezekiel 36.24-28	Psalms 42, 43
Ezekiel 37.1-14	Psalm 143
Zephaniah 3.14-20	Psalm 98
Romans 6.3-11	**Psalm 114**
Mark 16.1-8	

YEAR C

A minimum of three Old Testament readings should be chosen. The reading from Exodus 14 should always be used.

Genesis 1.1 – 2.4a	Psalm 136.1-9,23-26
Genesis 7.1-5,11-18; 8.6-18; 9.8-13	Psalm 46
Genesis 22.1-18	Psalm 16
Exodus 14.10-31; 15.20-21	*Canticle:* **Exodus 15.1b-13,17-18**
Isaiah 55.1-11	*Canticle:* Isaiah 12.2-6
Baruch 3.9-15,32 – 4.4	
or Proverbs 8.1-8,19-21; 9.4b-6	Psalm 19
Ezekiel 36.24-28	Psalms 42, 43
Ezekiel 37.1-14	Psalm 143
Zephaniah 3.14-20	Psalm 98
Romans 6.3-11	**Psalm 114**
Luke 24.1-12	

Easter Day

YEAR A	YEAR B	YEAR C
Principal Service		
Acts 10.34-43 *or* Jeremiah 31.1-6 Psalm 118.1-2,14-24* Colossians 3.1-4 *or* Acts 10.34-43 John 20.1-18 *or* Matthew 28.1-10	Acts 10.34-43 *or* Isaiah 25.6-9 Psalm 118.1-2,14-24* 1 Corinthians 15.1-11 *or* Acts 10.34-43 John 20.1-18 *or* Mark 16.1-8	Acts 10.34-43 *or* Isaiah 65.17-25 Psalm 118.1-2,14-24* 1 Corinthians 15.19-26 *or* Acts 10.34-43 John 20.1-18 *or* Luke 24.1-12
Second Service		
Psalms 114, 117 Song of Solomon 3.2-5; 8.6-7 John 20.11-18 if not read at the Principal Service *or* Revelation 1.12-18	Psalms 114, 117 Ezekiel 37.1-14 Luke 24.13-35	Psalms 66, 114, 117 Isaiah 43.1-21 1 Corinthians 15.1-11 *or* John 20.19-23
Third Service		
Psalm 105 *or* 66.1-12 Exodus 14.10-18,26 – 15.2 Revelation 15.2-4	Psalm 105 *or* 66.1-12 Genesis 1.1-5,26-31 2 Corinthians 5.14 – 6.2	Psalms 114, 117 Ezekiel 47.1-12 John 2.13-22

The Second Sunday of Easter

YEAR A	YEAR B	YEAR C
Principal Service		
Acts 2.14a,22-32 Psalm 16 1 Peter 1.3-9 John 20.19-31	Acts 4.32-35 Psalm 133 1 John 1.1 – 2.2 John 20.19-31	Acts 5.27-32 Psalm 118.14-29 *or* Psalm 150 Revelation 1.4-8 John 20.19-31
Second Service		
Psalm 30.1-5 Daniel 6.1-23 *or* 6.6-23 Mark 15.46 – 16.8	Psalm 143.1-11 Isaiah 26.1-9,19 Luke 24.1-12	Psalm 16 Isaiah 52.13 – 53.12 *or* 53.1-6,9-12 Luke 24.13-35
Third Service		
Psalm 81.1-10 Exodus 12.1-17 1 Corinthians 5.6b-8	Psalm 22.20-32 Isaiah 53.6-12 Romans 4.13-25	Psalm 136.1-16 Exodus 12.1-13 1 Peter 1.3-12

Old Testament Readings for Sundays in Eastertide

For those who require an Old Testament reading on the Sundays in Eastertide, provision is made in this table. If used, the reading from Acts must be used as the second reading.

Principal Service	
YEAR A	
The Second Sunday of Easter	Exodus 14.10-31; 15.20-21
The Third Sunday of Easter	Zephaniah 3.14-20
The Fourth Sunday of Easter	Genesis 7
The Fifth Sunday of Easter	Genesis 8.1-19
The Sixth Sunday of Easter	Genesis 8.20 – 9.17
The Seventh Sunday of Easter	Ezekiel 36.24-28
YEAR B	
The Second Sunday of Easter	Exodus 14.10-31; 15.20-21
The Third Sunday of Easter	Zephaniah 3.14-20
The Fourth Sunday of Easter	Genesis 7.1-5,11-18; 8.6-18; 9.8-13
The Fifth Sunday of Easter	Baruch 3.9-15,32 – 4.4
	or Genesis 22.1-18
The Sixth Sunday of Easter	Isaiah 55.1-11
The Seventh Sunday of Easter	Ezekiel 36.24-28
YEAR C	
The Second Sunday of Easter	Exodus 14.10-31; 15.20-21
The Third Sunday of Easter	Zephaniah 3.14-20
The Fourth Sunday of Easter	Genesis 7.1-5,11-18; 8.6-18; 9.8-13
The Fifth Sunday of Easter	Baruch 3.9-15,32 – 4.4
	or Genesis 22.1-18
The Sixth Sunday of Easter	Ezekiel 37.1-14
The Seventh Sunday of Easter	Ezekiel 36.24-28

The Third Sunday of Easter

YEAR A	YEAR B	YEAR C
Principal Service		
Acts 2.14a,36-41	Acts 3.12-19	Acts 9.1-6[7-20]
Psalm 116.1-4,12-19*	Psalm 4	Psalm 30
1 Peter 1.17-23	1 John 3.1-7	Revelation 5.11-14
Luke 24.13-35	Luke 24.36b-48	John 21.1-19
Second Service		
Psalm 48	Psalm 142	Psalm 86
Haggai 1.13 – 2.9	Deuteronomy 7.7-13	Isaiah 38.9-20
1 Corinthians 3.10-17	Revelation 2.1-11	John 11.[17-26]27-44
If the Second Service is a Eucharist, the following is read as a Gospel:	If the Second Service is a Eucharist, the following is read as a Gospel:	
John 2.13-22	Luke 16.19-31	
Third Service		
Psalm 23	Psalm 77.11-20	Psalm 80.1-7
Isaiah 40.1-11	Isaiah 63.7-15	Exodus 15.1-2,9-18
1 Peter 5.1-11	1 Corinthians 10.1-13	John 10.1-19

The Fourth Sunday of Easter

YEAR A	YEAR B	YEAR C
Principal Service		
Acts 2.42-47	Acts 4.5-12	Acts 9.36-43
Psalm 23	Psalm 23	Psalm 23
1 Peter 2.19-25	1 John 3.16-24	Revelation 7.9-17
John 10.1-10	John 10.11-18	John 10.22-30
Second Service		
Psalm 29.1-10	Psalm 81.8-16	Psalms 113, 114
Ezra 3.1-13	Exodus 16.4-15	Isaiah 63.7-14
Ephesians 2.11-22	Revelation 2.12-17	Luke 24.36-49
If the Second Service is a Eucharist, the following is read as a Gospel:	If the Second Service is a Eucharist, the following is read as a Gospel:	
Luke 19.37-48	John 6.30-40	
Third Service		
Psalm 106.6-24	Psalm 119.89-96	Psalm 146
Nehemiah 9.6-15	Nehemiah 8.1-12	1 Kings 17.17-24
1 Corinthians 10.1-13	Luke 24.25-32	Luke 7.11-23

The Fifth Sunday of Easter

YEAR A	YEAR B	YEAR C
Principal Service		
Acts 7.55-60	Acts 8.26-40	Acts 11.1-18
Psalm 31.1-5,15-16*	Psalm 22.25-31	Psalm 148*
1 Peter 2.2-10	1 John 4.7-21	Revelation 21.1-6
John 14.1-14	John 15.1-8	John 13.31-35
Second Service		
Psalm 147.1-11	Psalm 96	Psalm 98
Zechariah 4.1-10	Isaiah 60.1-14	Daniel 6.[1-5]6-23
Revelation 21.1-14	Revelation 3.1-13	Mark 15.46 – 16.8
If the Second Service is a Eucharist, the following is read as a Gospel:	If the Second Service is a Eucharist, the following is read as a Gospel:	
Luke 2.25-32[33-38]	Mark 16.9-16	
Third Service		
Psalm 30	Psalm 44.15-27	Psalm 16
Ezekiel 37.1-12	2 Maccabees 7.7-14 *or*	2 Samuel 7.4-13
John 5.19-29	Daniel 3.16-28	Acts 2.14a,22-32
	Hebrews 11.32 – 12.2	[33-36]

The Sixth Sunday of Easter

YEAR A	YEAR B	YEAR C
Principal Service		
Acts 17.22-31	Acts 10.44-48	Acts 16.9-15
Psalm 66.8-20	Psalm 98	Psalm 67
1 Peter 3.13-22	1 John 5.1-6	Revelation 21.10,22 – 22.5
John 14.15-21	John 15.9-17	John 14.23-29 *or* John 5.1-9
Second Service		
Psalms 87, 36.5-10	Psalm 45	Psalms 126, 127
Zechariah 8.1-13	Song of Solomon 4.16 – 5.2; 8.6-7	Zephaniah 3.14-20
Revelation 21.22 – 22.5	Revelation 3.14-22	Matthew 28.1-10, 16-20
If the Second Service is a Eucharist, the following is read as a Gospel:	If the Second Service is a Eucharist, the following is read as a Gospel:	
John 21.1-14	Luke 22.24-30	
Third Service		
Psalm 73.21-28	Psalm 104.26-32	Psalm 40.1-8
Job 14.1-2,7-15; 19.23-27a	Ezekiel 47.1-12	Genesis 1.26-28 [29-31]
1 Thessalonians 4.13-18	John 21.1-19	Colossians 3.1-11

Ascension Day

Evening Prayer on the Eve Years A, B, C
Psalms 15, 24 2 Samuel 23.1-5 Colossians 2.20 – 3.4

YEAR A	YEAR B	YEAR C
Principal Service *(Readings for Years A, B, C are the same)*		
The reading from Acts must be used as either the first or second reading.		

Acts 1.1-11 *or*
  Daniel 7.9-14
Psalm 47 *or* Psalm 93
Ephesians 1.15-23 *or*
  Acts 1.1-11
Luke 24.44-53
	Acts 1.1-11 *or*
	  Daniel 7.9-14
	Psalm 47 *or* Psalm 93
	Ephesians 1.15-23 *or*
	  Acts 1.1-11
	Luke 24.44-53
		Acts 1.1-11 *or*
		  Daniel 7.9-14
		Psalm 47 *or* Psalm 93
		Ephesians 1.15-23 *or*
		  Acts 1.1-11
		Luke 24.44-53

Second Service		

Psalm 8
Song of the Three
  29-37 *or*
  2 Kings 2.1-15
Revelation 5
If the Second Service is a Eucharist, the following is read as a Gospel:
Mark 16.14-20
	Psalm 8
	Song of the Three
	  29-37 *or*
	  2 Kings 2.1-15
	Revelation 5
	If the Second Service is a Eucharist, the following is read as a Gospel:
	Matthew 28.16-20
		Psalm 8
		Song of the Three
		  29-37 *or*
		  2 Kings 2.1-15
		Revelation 5
		If the Second Service is a Eucharist, the following is read as a Gospel:
		Matthew 28.16-20

Third Service		

Psalm 110
Isaiah 52.7-15
Hebrews 7.11-28 (*or*
  7.26-28)
	Psalm 110
	Isaiah 52.7-15
	Hebrews 7.[11-25]
	  26-28
		Psalm 110
		Isaiah 52.7-15
		Hebrews 7.[11-25]
		  26-28

The Seventh Sunday of Easter
Sunday after Ascension Day

YEAR A	YEAR B	YEAR C
Principal Service		
Acts 1.6-14	Acts 1.15-17,21-26	Acts 16.16-34
Psalm 68.1-10,32-35*	Psalm 1	Psalm 97
1 Peter 4.12-14; 5.6-11	1 John 5.9-13	Revelation 22.12-14,
John 17.1-11	John 17.6-19	16-17,20-21
		John 17.20-26
Second Service		
Psalm 47	Psalm 147.1-11	Psalm 68*
2 Samuel 23.1-5	Isaiah 61.1-11	Isaiah 44.1-8
Ephesians 1.15-23	Luke 4.14-21	Ephesians 4.7-16
If the Second Service is a Eucharist, the following is read as a Gospel:		If the Second Service is a Eucharist, the following is read as a Gospel:
Mark 16.14-20		Luke 24.44-53
Third Service		
Psalm 104.26-37	Psalm 76	Psalm 99
Isaiah 65.17-25	Isaiah 14.3-15	Deuteronomy 34
Revelation 21.1-8	Revelation 14.1-13	Luke 24.44-53 or
		Acts 1.1-8

Day of Pentecost
Whit Sunday

YEAR A	YEAR B	YEAR C
Evening Prayer on the Eve		
Psalm 48	Psalm 48	Psalm 48
Deuteronomy 16.9-15	Deuteronomy 16.9-15	Deuteronomy 16.9-15
John 15.26 – 16.15	John 7.37-39	John 7.37-39

YEAR A	YEAR B	YEAR C
Principal Service		
The reading from Acts must be used as either the first or second reading.	*The reading from Acts must be used as either the first or second reading.*	*The reading from Acts must be used as either the first or second reading.*
Acts 2.1-21 *or*	Acts 2.1-21 *or*	Acts 2.1-21 *or*
Numbers 11.24-30	Ezekiel 37.1-14	Genesis 11.1-9
Psalm 104.24-34,35b*	Psalm 104.24-34,35b*	Psalm 104.24-34,35b*
1 Corinthians 12.3b-13 *or* Acts 2.1-21	Romans 8.22-27 *or* Acts 2.1-21	Romans 8.14-17 *or* Acts 2.1-21
John 20.19-23 *or*	John 15.26-27;	John 14.8-17[25-27]
John 7.37-39	16.4b-15	
Second Service		
Psalms 67, 133	Psalm 139.1-12	Psalms 36.5-10; 150
Joel 2.21-32	[13-18,23-24]	Exodus 33.7-20
Acts 2.14-21[22-38]	Ezekiel 36.22-28	2 Corinthians 3.4-18
If the Second Service is a Eucharist, the following is read as a Gospel:	Acts 2.22-38	If the Second Service is a Eucharist, the following is read as a Gospel:
Luke 24.44-53	If the Second Service is a Eucharist, the following is read as a Gospel:	John 16.4b-15
	John 20.19-23	
Third Service		
Psalm 87	Psalm 145	Psalm 33.1-12
Genesis 11.1-9	Isaiah 11.1-9 *or*	Isaiah 40.12-23 *or*
Acts 10.34-48	Wisdom 7.15-23 [24-27]	Wisdom 9.9-17
	1 Corinthians 12.4-13	1 Corinthians 2.6-16

Trinity Sunday

YEAR A	YEAR B	YEAR C
Evening Prayer on the Eve		
Psalms 97, 98	Psalms 97, 98	Psalms 97, 98
Exodus 34.1-10	Isaiah 40.12-31	Isaiah 40.12-31
Mark 1.1-13	Mark 1.1-13	Mark 1.1-13

YEAR A	YEAR B	YEAR C
Principal Service		
Isaiah 40.12-17,27-31	Isaiah 6.1-8	Proverbs 8.1-4,22-31
Psalm 8	Psalm 29	Psalm 8
2 Corinthians 13.11-13	Romans 8.12-17	Romans 5.1-5
Matthew 28.16-20	John 3.1-17	John 16.12-15
Second Service		
Psalms 93, 150	Psalm 104.1-9	Psalm 73.1-3,16-28
Isaiah 6.1-8	Ezekiel 1.4-10,22-28a	Exodus 3.1-15
John 16.5-15	Revelation 4.1-11	John 3.1-17
	If the Second Service is a Eucharist, the following is read as a Gospel:	
	Mark 1.1-13	
Third Service		
Psalm 86.8-13	Psalm 33.1-12	Psalm 29
Exodus 3.1-6,13-15	Proverbs 8.1-4,22-31	Isaiah 6.1-8
John 17.1-11	2 Corinthians 13.[5-10] 11-13	Revelation 4

If the Sunday between 24 and 28 May inclusive follows Trinity Sunday, Proper 3 (page 49) is used.

Day of Thanksgiving for Holy Communion
Thursday after Trinity Sunday (Corpus Christi)

Evening Prayer on the Eve (if required)		
	Psalms 110, 111	
	Exodus 16.2-15	
	John 6.22-35	

Eucharist	Morning Prayer	Evening Prayer
Genesis 14.18-20	Psalm 147	Psalms 23, 42, 43
Psalm 116.12-19	Deuteronomy 8.2-16	Proverbs 9.1-5
1 Corinthians 11.23-26	1 Corinthians 10.1-17	Luke 9.11-17
John 6.51-58		

Proper 4

Sunday between 29 May and 4 June inclusive (if after Trinity Sunday)

YEAR A	YEAR B	YEAR C
Principal Service		
CONTINUOUS	CONTINUOUS	CONTINUOUS
Genesis 6.9-22; 7.24; 8.14-19	1 Samuel 3.1-10 [11-20]	1 Kings 18.20-21 [22-29]30-39
Psalm 46	Psalm 139.1-6,13-18	Psalm 96
Romans 1.16-17; 3.22b-28[29-31]	2 Corinthians 4.5-12	Galatians 1.1-12
Matthew 7.21-29	Mark 2.23 – 3.6	Luke 7.1-10
	or	
RELATED	RELATED	RELATED
Deuteronomy 11.18-21,26-28	Deuteronomy 5.12-15	1 Kings 8.22-23,41-43
Psalm 31.1-5,19-24*	Psalm 81.1-10	Psalm 96.1-9
Romans 1.16-17; 3.22b-28[29-31]	2 Corinthians 4.5-12	Galatians 1.1-12
Matthew 7.21-29	Mark 2.23 – 3.6	Luke 7.1-10
Second Service		
Psalm 33*	Psalm 35*	Psalm 39
Ruth 2.1-20a	Jeremiah 5.1-19	Genesis 4.1-16
Luke 8.4-15	Romans 7.7-25	Mark 3.7-19
	If the Second Service is a Eucharist, the following is read as a Gospel:	
	Luke 7.1-10	
Third Service		
Psalm 37.1-18	Psalms 28, 32	Psalm 41
Deuteronomy 5.1-21	Deuteronomy 5.1-21	Deuteronomy 5.1-21
Acts 21.17-39a	Acts 21.17-39a	Acts 21.17-39a

Proper 5

Sunday between 5 and 11 June inclusive (if after Trinity Sunday)

YEAR A	YEAR B	YEAR C
Principal Service		
CONTINUOUS	CONTINUOUS	CONTINUOUS
Genesis 12.1-9	1 Samuel 8.4-11[12-15]16-20[11.14-15]	1 Kings 17.8-16[17-24]
Psalm 33.1-12	Psalm 138	Psalm 146
Romans 4.13-25	2 Corinthians 4.13 – 5.1	Galatians 1.11-24
Matthew 9.9-13,18-26	Mark 3.20-35	Luke 7.11-17
	or	
RELATED	RELATED	RELATED
Hosea 5.15 – 6.6	Genesis 3.8-15	1 Kings 17.17-24
Psalm 50.7-15	Psalm 130	Psalm 30
Romans 4.13-25	2 Corinthians 4.13 – 5.1	Galatians 1.11-24
Matthew 9.9-13,18-26	Mark 3.20-35	Luke 7.11-17
Second Service		
Psalms [39] 41	Psalm 37.1-11[12-14]	Psalm 44*
1 Samuel 18.1-16	Jeremiah 6.16-21	Genesis 8.15 – 9.17
Luke 8.41-56	Romans 9.1-13	Mark 4.1-20
	If the Second Service is a Eucharist, the following is read as a Gospel:	
	Luke 7.11-17	
Third Service		
Psalm 38	Psalm 36	Psalm 45
Deuteronomy 6.10-25	Deuteronomy 6.10-25	Deuteronomy 6.10-25
Acts 22.22 – 23.11	Acts 22.22 – 23.11	Acts 22.22 – 23.11

Proper 6

Sunday between 12 and 18 June inclusive (if after Trinity Sunday)

YEAR A	YEAR B	YEAR C
Principal Service		
CONTINUOUS	CONTINUOUS	CONTINUOUS
Genesis 18.1-15 [21.1-7]	1 Samuel 15.34 – 16.13	1 Kings 21.1-10[11-14] 15-21a
Psalm 116.1-2,12-19*	Psalm 20	Psalm 5.1-8
Romans 5.1-8	2 Corinthians 5.6-10 [11-13]14-17	Galatians 2.15-21
Matthew 9.35 – 10.8 [9-23]	Mark 4.26-34	Luke 7.36 – 8.3
	or	
RELATED	RELATED	RELATED
Exodus 19.2-8a	Ezekiel 17.22-24	2 Samuel 11.26 – 12.10,13-15
Psalm 100	Psalm 92.1-4,12-15*	Psalm 32
Romans 5.1-8	2 Corinthians 5.6-10 [11-13]14-17	Galatians 2.15-21
Matthew 9.35 – 10.8 [9-23]	Mark 4.26-34	Luke 7.36 – 8.3
Second Service		
Psalms [42] 43	Psalm 39	Psalms 52 [53]
1 Samuel 21.1-15	Jeremiah 7.1-16	Genesis 13
Luke 11.14-28	Romans 9.14-26	Mark 4.21-41
	If the Second Service is a Eucharist, the following is read as a Gospel:	
	Luke 7.36 – 8.3	
Third Service		
Psalm 45	Psalms 42, 43	Psalm 49
Deuteronomy 10.12 – 11.1	Deuteronomy 10.12 – 11.1	Deuteronomy 10.12 – 11.1
Acts 23.12-35	Acts 23.12-35	Acts 23.12-35

Proper 7

Sunday between 19 and 25 June inclusive (if after Trinity Sunday)

YEAR A	YEAR B	YEAR C
Principal Service		
CONTINUOUS	CONTINUOUS	CONTINUOUS

Genesis 21.8-21
Psalm 86.1-10,16-17*
Romans 6.1b-11
Matthew 10.24-39
	1 Samuel 17.[1a,4-11,
	  19-23]32-49
	Psalm 9.9-20
	Or:
	1 Samuel 17.57 – 18.5,
	  10-16
	Psalm 133
	2 Corinthians 6.1-13
	Mark 4.35-41
	or
		1 Kings 19.1-4[5-7]
		  8-15a
		Psalms 42, 43*
		Galatians 3.23-29
		Luke 8.26-39

RELATED	RELATED	RELATED
Jeremiah 20.7-13 Psalm 69.7-10[11-15] 16-18* Romans 6.1b-11 Matthew 10.24-39	Job 38.1-11 Psalm 107.1-3,23-32* 2 Corinthians 6.1-13 Mark 4.35-41	Isaiah 65.1-9 Psalm 22.19-28 Galatians 3.23-29 Luke 8.26-39
Second Service		
Psalms 46 [48] 1 Samuel 24.1-17 Luke 14.12-24	Psalm 49 Jeremiah 10.1-16 Romans 11.25-36 If the Second Service is a Eucharist, the following is read as a Gospel: Luke 8.26-39	Psalms [50] 57 Genesis 24.1-27 Mark 5.21-43
Third Service		
Psalm 49 Deuteronomy 11.1-15 Acts 27.1-12	Psalm 48 Deuteronomy 11.1-15 Acts 27.1-12	Psalm 55.1-14,16-19 Deuteronomy 11.1-15 Acts 27.1-12

Proper 8

Sunday between 26 June and 2 July inclusive

YEAR A	YEAR B	YEAR C
Principal Service		
CONTINUOUS	CONTINUOUS	CONTINUOUS
Genesis 22.1-14	2 Samuel 1.1,17-27	2 Kings 2.1-2,6-14
Psalm 13	Psalm 130	Psalm 77.1-2,11-20*
Romans 6.12-23	2 Corinthians 8.7-15	Galatians 5.1,13-25
Matthew 10.40-42	Mark 5.21-43	Luke 9.51-62
	or	
RELATED	RELATED	RELATED
Jeremiah 28.5-9	Wisdom of Solomon	1 Kings 19.15-16,
Psalm 89.1-4,15-18*	1.13-15; 2.23-24	19-21
Romans 6.12-23	*Canticle:* Lamentations	Psalm 16
Matthew 10.40-42	3.23-33 *or* Psalm 30	Galatians 5.1,13-25
	2 Corinthians 8.7-15	Luke 9.51-62
	Mark 5.21-43	
	Lamentations 3.23-33	
	may be read as the first	
	reading in place of	
	Wisdom 1.13-15; 2.23-	
	24.	
Second Service		
Psalm 50*	Psalms [52] 53	Psalms [59.1-5,16-17]
1 Samuel 28.3-19	Jeremiah 11.1-14	60
Luke 17.20-37	Romans 13.1-10	Genesis 27.1-40
	If the Second Service is a Eucharist, the following is read as a Gospel:	Mark 6.1-6
	Luke 9.51-62	
Third Service		
Psalms 52, 53	Psalm 56	Psalm 64
Deuteronomy 15.1-11	Deuteronomy 15.1-11	Deuteronomy 15.1-11
Acts 27.13-44 (*or*	Acts 27.[13-32]33-44	Acts 27.[13-32]33-44
27.33-44)		

Proper 9

Sunday between 3 and 9 July inclusive

YEAR A	YEAR B	YEAR C
Principal Service		
CONTINUOUS	CONTINUOUS	CONTINUOUS
Genesis 24.34-38, 42-49,58-67 Psalm 45.10-17 *or* *Canticle:* Song of Solomon 2.8-13 Romans 7.15-25a Matthew 11.16-19, 25-30	2 Samuel 5.1-5,9-10 Psalm 48 2 Corinthians 12.2-10 Mark 6.1-13	2 Kings 5.1-14 Psalm 30 Galatians 6.[1-6]7-16 Luke 10.1-11,16-20
	or	
RELATED	RELATED	RELATED
Zechariah 9.9-12 Psalm 145.8-14 Romans 7.15-25a Matthew 11.16-19, 25-30	Ezekiel 2.1-5 Psalm 123 2 Corinthians 12.2-10 Mark 6.1-13	Isaiah 66.10-14 Psalm 66.1-9 Galatians 6.[1-6]7-16 Luke 10.1-11,16-20
Second Service		
Psalms 56 [57] 2 Samuel 2.1-11; 3.1 Luke 18.31 – 19.10	Psalms [63] 64 Jeremiah 20.1-11a Romans 14.1-17 If the Second Service is a Eucharist, the following is read as a Gospel: Luke 10.1-11,16-20	Psalms 65 [70] Genesis 29.1-20 Mark 6.7-29
Third Service		
Psalm 55.1-15,18-22 Deuteronomy 24.10-22 Acts 28.1-16	Psalm 57 Deuteronomy 24.10-22 Acts 28.1-16	Psalm 74 Deuteronomy 24.10-22 Acts 28.1-16

Proper 10

Sunday between 10 and 16 July inclusive

YEAR A	YEAR B	YEAR C
Principal Service		
CONTINUOUS	CONTINUOUS	CONTINUOUS
Genesis 25.19-34	2 Samuel 6.1-5,12b-19	Amos 7.7-17
Psalm 119.105-112	Psalm 24	Psalm 82
Romans 8.1-11	Ephesians 1.3-14	Colossians 1.1-14
Matthew 13.1-9,18-23	Mark 6.14-29	Luke 10.25-37
	or	
RELATED	RELATED	RELATED
Isaiah 55.10-13	Amos 7.7-15	Deuteronomy 30.9-14
Psalm 65.[1-8]9-13*	Psalm 85.8-13	Psalm 25.1-10
Romans 8.1-11	Ephesians 1.3-14	Colossians 1.1-14
Matthew 13.1-9,18-23	Mark 6.14-29	Luke 10.25-37
Second Service		
Psalms 60 [63]	Psalm 66*	Psalm 77*
2 Samuel 7.18-29	Job 4.1; 5.6-27 *or*	Genesis 32.9-30
Luke 19.41 – 20.8	Ecclesiasticus 4.11-31	Mark 7.1-23
	Romans 15.14-29	
	If the Second Service is a Eucharist, the following is read as a Gospel:	
	Luke 10.25-37	
Third Service		
Psalms 64, 65	Psalm 65	Psalm 76
Deuteronomy 28.1-14	Deuteronomy 28.1-14	Deuteronomy 28.1-14
Acts 28.17-30	Acts 28.17-30	Acts 28.17-31

Proper 11

Sunday between 17 and 23 July inclusive

YEAR A	YEAR B	YEAR C
Principal Service		
CONTINUOUS	CONTINUOUS	CONTINUOUS
Genesis 28.10-19a Psalm 139.1-12,23-24* Romans 8.12-25 Matthew 13.24-30, 36-43	2 Samuel 7.1-14a Psalm 89.20-37 Ephesians 2.11-22 Mark 6.30-34,53-56	Amos 8.1-12 Psalm 52 Colossians 1.15-28 Luke 10.38-42
	or	
RELATED	RELATED	RELATED

Wisdom of Solomon
    12.13,16-19 *or*
    Isaiah 44.6-8
Psalm 86.11-17
Romans 8.12-25
Matthew 13.24-30,
    36-43
	Jeremiah 23.1-6
	Psalm 23
	Ephesians 2.11-22
	Mark 6.30-34,53-56
		Genesis 18.1-10a
		Psalm 15
		Colossians 1.15-28
		Luke 10.38-42

Second Service		

Psalms 67 [70]
1 Kings 2.10-12;
    3.16-28
Acts 4.1-22
If the Second Service is a
Eucharist, the following is read as
a Gospel:
Mark 6.30-34,53-56
	Psalm 73*
	Job 13.13 – 14.6 *or*
	    Ecclesiasticus 18.1-14
	Hebrews 2.5-18
	If the Second Service is a
	Eucharist, the following is read as
	a Gospel:
	Luke 10.38-42
		Psalm 81
		Genesis 41.1-16,25-37
		1 Corinthians 4.8-13
		If the Second Service is a
		Eucharist, the following is read as
		a Gospel:
		John 4.31-35

Third Service		
Psalm 71 Deuteronomy 30.1-10 1 Peter 3.8-18	Psalms 67, 70 Deuteronomy 30.1-10 1 Peter 3.8-18	Psalms 82, 100 Deuteronomy 30.1-10 1 Peter 3.8-18

Proper 12

Sunday between 24 and 30 July inclusive

YEAR A	YEAR B	YEAR C
Principal Service		
CONTINUOUS	CONTINUOUS	CONTINUOUS

Genesis 29.15-28
Psalm 105.1-11,45b*
  or Psalm 128
Romans 8.26-39
Matthew 13.31-33,
  44-52
	2 Samuel 11.1-15
	Psalm 14
	Ephesians 3.14-21
	John 6.1-21
		Hosea 1.2-10
		Psalm 85*
		Colossians 2.6-15
		  [16-19]
		Luke 11.1-13

	or	
RELATED	RELATED	RELATED

1 Kings 3.5-12
Psalm 119.129-136
Romans 8.26-39
Matthew 13.31-33,
  44-52
	2 Kings 4.42-44
	Psalm 145.10-18
	Ephesians 3.14-21
	John 6.1-21
		Genesis 18.20-32
		Psalm 138
		Colossians 2.6-15
		  [16-19]
		Luke 11.1-13

Second Service		

Psalms 75 [76]
1 Kings 6.11-14,23-38
Acts 12.1-17
If the Second Service is a
Eucharist, the following is read as
a Gospel:
John 6.1-21
	Psalm 74*
	Job 19.1-27a *or*
	  Ecclesiasticus 38.24-
	  34
	Hebrews 8
	If the Second Service is a
	Eucharist, the following is read as
	a Gospel:
	Luke 11.1-13
		Psalm 88*
		Genesis 42.1-25
		1 Corinthians 10.1-24
		If the Second Service is a
		Eucharist, the following is read as
		a Gospel:
		Matthew 13.24-30
		  [31-43]

Third Service		

Psalm 77
Song of Solomon 2 *or*
  1 Maccabees 2.[1-14]
  15-22
1 Peter 4.7-14
	Psalm 75
	Song of Solomon 2 *or*
	  1 Maccabees 2.[1-14]
	  15-22
	1 Peter 4.7-14
		Psalm 95
		Song of Solomon 2 *or*
		  1 Maccabees 2.[1-14]
		  15-22
		1 Peter 4.7-14

Proper 13

Sunday between 31 July and 6 August inclusive

YEAR A	YEAR B	YEAR C
Principal Service		
CONTINUOUS	CONTINUOUS	CONTINUOUS
Genesis 32.22-31	2 Samuel 11.26 –	Hosea 11.1-11
Psalm 17.1-7,15*	12.13a	Psalm 107.1-9,43*
Romans 9.1-5	Psalm 51.1-12	Colossians 3.1-11
Matthew 14.13-21	Ephesians 4.1-16	Luke 12.13-21
	John 6.24-35	
	or	
RELATED	RELATED	RELATED
Isaiah 55.1-5	Exodus 16.2-4,9-15	Ecclesiastes 1.2,12-14;
Psalm 145.8-9,14-21*	Psalm 78.23-29	2.18-23
Romans 9.1-5	Ephesians 4.1-16	Psalm 49.1-12*
Matthew 14.13-21	John 6.24-35	Colossians 3.1-11
		Luke 12.13-21
Second Service		
Psalm 80*	Psalm 88*	Psalm 107.1-32*
1 Kings 10.1-13	Job 28 *or* Ecclesiasticus	Genesis 50.4-26
Acts 13.1-13	42.15-25	1 Corinthians 14.1-19
If the Second Service is a Eucharist, the following is read as a Gospel:	Hebrews 11.17-31	If the Second Service is a Eucharist, the following is read as a Gospel:
John 6.24-35	If the Second Service is a Eucharist, the following is read as a Gospel:	Mark 6.45-52
	Luke 12.13-21	
Third Service		
Psalm 85	Psalm 86	Psalm 106.1-10
Song of Solomon 5.2-	Song of Solomon 5.2-	Song of Solomon 5.2-
16 *or*	16 *or*	16 *or*
1 Maccabees 3.1-12	1 Maccabees 3.1-12	1 Maccabees 3.1-12
2 Peter 1.1-15	2 Peter 1.1-15	2 Peter 1.1-15

Proper 14

Sunday between 7 and 13 August inclusive

YEAR A	YEAR B	YEAR C
Principal Service		
CONTINUOUS	CONTINUOUS	CONTINUOUS
Genesis 37.1-4,12-28 Psalm 105.1-6,16-22, 45b* Romans 10.5-15 Matthew 14.22-33	2 Samuel 18.5-9,15, 31-33 Psalm 130 Ephesians 4.25 – 5.2 John 6.35,41-51 or	Isaiah 1.1,10-20 Psalm 50.1-8, 22-23* Hebrews 11.1-3,8-16 Luke 12.32-40
RELATED	RELATED	RELATED
1 Kings 19.9-18 Psalm 85.8-13 Romans 10.5-15 Matthew 14.22-33	1 Kings 19.4-8 Psalm 34.1-8 Ephesians 4.25 – 5.2 John 6.35,41-51	Genesis 15.1-6 Psalm 33.12-22* Hebrews 11.1-3,8-16 Luke 12.32-40
Second Service		
Psalm 86 1 Kings 11.41 – 12.20 Acts 14.8-20 If the Second Service is a Eucharist, the following is read as a Gospel: John 6.35,41-51	Psalm 91* Job 39.1 – 40.4 *or* Ecclesiasticus 43.13-33 Hebrews 12.1-17 If the Second Service is a Eucharist, the following is read as a Gospel: Luke 12.32-40	Psalms 108 [116] Isaiah 11.10 – 12.6 2 Corinthians 1.1-22 If the Second Service is a Eucharist, the following is read as a Gospel: Mark 7.24-30
Third Service		
Psalm 88 Song of Solomon 8.5-7 *or* 1 Maccabees 14.4-15 2 Peter 3.8-13	Psalm 90 Song of Solomon 8.5-7 *or* 1 Maccabees 14.4-15 2 Peter 3.8-13	Psalm 115 Song of Solomon 8.5-7 *or* 1 Maccabees 14.4-15 2 Peter 3.8-13

Proper 15

Sunday between 14 and 20 August inclusive

YEAR A	YEAR B	YEAR C
Principal Service		
CONTINUOUS	CONTINUOUS	CONTINUOUS
Genesis 45.1-15	1 Kings 2.10-12; 3.3-	Isaiah 5.1-7
Psalm 133	14	Psalm 80.1-2,8-19*
Romans 11.1-2a, 29-32	Psalm 111	Hebrews 11.29 – 12.2
Matthew 15.[10-20]	Ephesians 5.15-20	Luke 12.49-56
21-28	John 6.51-58	
	or	
RELATED	RELATED	RELATED
Isaiah 56.1,6-8	Proverbs 9.1-6	Jeremiah 23.23-29
Psalm 67	Psalm 34.9-14	Psalm 82
Romans 11.1-2a,29-32	Ephesians 5.15-20	Hebrews 11.29 – 12.2
Matthew 15.[10-20]	John 6.51-58	Luke 12.49-56
21-28		
Second Service		
Psalm 90*	Psalms [92] 100	Psalm 119.17-32*
2 Kings 4.1-37	Exodus 2.23 – 3.10	Isaiah 28.9-22
Acts 16.1-15	Hebrews 13.1-15	2 Corinthians 8.1-9
If the Second Service is a Eucharist, the following is read as a Gospel:	If the Second Service is a Eucharist, the following is read as a Gospel:	If the Second Service is a Eucharist, the following is read as a Gospel:
John 6.51-58	Luke 12.49-56	Matthew 20.1-16
Third Service		
Psalm 92	Psalm 106.1-10	Psalm 119.33-48
Jonah 1 *or*	Jonah 1 *or*	Jonah 1 *or*
Ecclesiasticus 3.1-15	Ecclesiasticus 3.1-15	Ecclesiasticus 3.1-15
2 Peter 3.14-18	2 Peter 3.14-18	2 Peter 3.14-18

Proper 16

Sunday between 21 and 27 August inclusive

YEAR A	YEAR B	YEAR C
Principal Service		
CONTINUOUS	CONTINUOUS	CONTINUOUS
Exodus 1.8 – 2.10	1 Kings 8.[1,6,10-11]	Jeremiah 1.4-10
Psalm 124	22-30,41-43	Psalm 71.1-6
Romans 12.1-8	Psalm 84	Hebrews 12.18-29
Matthew 16.13-20	Ephesians 6.10-20	Luke 13.10-17
	John 6.56-69	
	or	
RELATED	RELATED	RELATED
Isaiah 51.1-6	Joshua 24.1-2a,14-18	Isaiah 58.9b-14
Psalm 138	Psalm 34.15-22	Psalm 103.1-8
Romans 12.1-8	Ephesians 6.10-20	Hebrews 12.18-29
Matthew 16.13-20	John 6.56-69	Luke 13.10-17
Second Service		
Psalm 95	Psalm 116*	Psalm 119.49-72*
2 Kings 6.8-23	Exodus 4.27 – 5.1	Isaiah 30.8-21
Acts 17.15-34	Hebrews 13.16-21	2 Corinthians 9
If the Second Service is a Eucharist, the following is read as a Gospel:	If the Second Service is a Eucharist, the following is read as a Gospel:	If the Second Service is a Eucharist, the following is read as a Gospel:
John 6.56-69	Luke 13.10-17	Matthew 21.28-32
Third Service		
Psalm 104.1-25	Psalm 115	Psalm 119.73-88
Jonah 2 *or*	Jonah 2 *or*	Jonah 2 *or*
Ecclesiasticus 3.17-29	Ecclesiasticus 3.17-29	Ecclesiasticus 3.17-29
Revelation 1	Revelation 1	Revelation 1

Proper 17

Sunday between 28 August and 3 September inclusive

YEAR A	YEAR B	YEAR C
Principal Service		
CONTINUOUS	CONTINUOUS	CONTINUOUS

Exodus 3.1-15
Psalm 105.1-6,23-26,
  45c*
Romans 12.9-21
Matthew 16.21-28
	Song of Solomon 2.8-
	  13
	Psalm 45.1-2,6-9*
	James 1.17-27
	Mark 7.1-8,14-15,
	  21-23
	
	or
		Jeremiah 2.4-13
		Psalm 81.1,10-16*
		Hebrews 13.1-8,15-16
		Luke 14.1,7-14

RELATED	RELATED	RELATED

Jeremiah 15.15-21
Psalm 26.1-8
Romans 12.9-21
Matthew 16.21-28
	Deuteronomy 4.1-2,
	  6-9
	Psalm 15
	James 1.17-27
	Mark 7.1-8,14-15,
	  21-23
		Ecclesiasticus 10.12-18
		  or Proverbs 25.6-7
		Psalm 112
		Hebrews 13.1-8,15-16
		Luke 14.1,7-14

Second Service		

Psalm 105.1-15
2 Kings 6.24-25;
  7.3-20
Acts 18.1-16
<small>If the Second Service is a
Eucharist, the following is read as
a Gospel:</small>
Mark 7.1-8,14-15,
  21-23
	Psalm 119.1-16*
	Exodus 12.21-27
	Matthew 4.23 – 5.20
		Psalm 119.81-96*
		Isaiah 33.13-22
		John 3.22-36

Third Service		

Psalm 107.1-32
Jonah 3.1-9 *or*
  Ecclesiasticus 11.7-28
  (*or* 19-28)
Revelation 3.14-22
	Psalm 119.17-40
	Jonah 3.1-9 *or*
	  Ecclesiasticus 11.7-28
	  (*or* 19-28)
	Revelation 3.14-22
		Psalm 119.161-176
		Jonah 3.1-9 *or*
		  Ecclesiasticus 11.[7-
		  17]18-28
		Revelation 3.14-22

Proper 18

Sunday between 4 and 10 September inclusive

YEAR A	YEAR B	YEAR C
Principal Service		
CONTINUOUS	CONTINUOUS	CONTINUOUS
Exodus 12.1-14 Psalm 149 Romans 13.8-14 Matthew 18.15-20	Proverbs 22.1-2,8-9, 22-23 Psalm 125 James 2.1-10[11-13] 14-17 Mark 7.24-37 or	Jeremiah 18.1-11 Psalm 139.1-6,13-18* Philemon 1-21 Luke 14.25-33
RELATED	RELATED	RELATED
Ezekiel 33.7-11 Psalm 119.33-40 Romans 13.8-14 Matthew 18.15-20	Isaiah 35.4-7a Psalm 146 James 2.1-10[11-13] 14-17 Mark 7.24-37	Deuteronomy 30.15- 20 Psalm 1 Philemon 1-21 Luke 14.25-33
Second Service		
Psalm 108 [115] Ezekiel 12.21 – 13.16 Acts 19.1-20 If the Second Service is a Eucharist, the following is read as a Gospel: Mark 7.24-37	Psalm 119.41-56* Exodus 14.5-31 Matthew 6.1-18	Psalms [120] 121 Isaiah 43.14 – 44.5 John 5.30-47
Third Service		
Psalm 119.17-32 Jonah 3.10 – 4.11 *or* Ecclesiasticus 27.30 – 28.9 Revelation 8.1-5	Psalm 119.57-72 Jonah 3.10 – 4.11 *or* Ecclesiasticus 27.30 – 28.9 Revelation 8.1-5	Psalms 122, 123 Jonah 3.10 – 4.11 *or* Ecclesiasticus 27.30 – 28.9 Revelation 8.1-5

Proper 19

Sunday between 11 and 17 September inclusive

YEAR A	YEAR B	YEAR C
Principal Service		
CONTINUOUS	CONTINUOUS	CONTINUOUS

Exodus 14.19-31
Psalm 114 *or*
  Canticle: Exodus
  15.1b-11, 20-21
Romans 14.1-12
Matthew 18.21-35
	Proverbs 1.20-33
	Psalm 19* *or*
	  Canticle: Wisdom of
	  Solomon 7.26 – 8.1
	James 3.1-12
	Mark 8.27-38
	                or
		Jeremiah 4.11-12,
		  22-28
		Psalm 14
		1 Timothy 1.12-17
		Luke 15.1-10

RELATED	RELATED	RELATED
Genesis 50.15-21 Psalm 103.[1-7]8-13* Romans 14.1-12 Matthew 18.21-35	Isaiah 50.4-9a Psalm 116.1-9 James 3.1-12 Mark 8.27-38	Exodus 32.7-14 Psalm 51.1-10 1 Timothy 1.12-17 Luke 15.1-10
Second Service		
Psalm 119.41-48 [49-64] Ezekiel 20.1-8,33-44 Acts 20.17-38 If the Second Service is a Eucharist, the following is read as a Gospel: Mark 8.27-38	Psalm 119.73-88* Exodus 18.13-26 Matthew 7.1-14	Psalms 124, 125 Isaiah 60 John 6.51-69
Third Service		
Psalm 119.65-88 Isaiah 44.24 – 45.8 Revelation 12.1-12	Psalm 119.105-120 Isaiah 44.24 – 45.8 Revelation 12.1-12	Psalms 126, 127 Isaiah 44.24 – 45.8 Revelation 12.1-12

Proper 20

Sunday between 18 and 24 September inclusive

YEAR A	YEAR B	YEAR C
Principal Service		
CONTINUOUS	CONTINUOUS	CONTINUOUS
Exodus 16.2-15	Proverbs 31.10-31	Jeremiah 8.18 – 9.1
Psalm 105.1-6,37-45*	Psalm 1	Psalm 79.1-9
Philippians 1.21-30	James 3.13 – 4.3,7-8a	1 Timothy 2.1-7
Matthew 20.1-16	Mark 9.30-37	Luke 16.1-13
	or	
RELATED	RELATED	RELATED
Jonah 3.10 – 4.11	Wisdom of Solomon	Amos 8.4-7
Psalm 145.1-8	1.16 – 2.1,12-22 *or*	Psalm 113
Philippians 1.21-30	Jeremiah 11.18-20	1 Timothy 2.1-7
Matthew 20.1-16	Psalm 54	Luke 16.1-13
	James 3.13 – 4.3,7-8a	
	Mark 9.30-37	
Second Service		
Psalm 119.113-136*	Psalm 119.137-152*	Psalms [128] 129
Ezekiel 33.23,30 – 34.10	Exodus 19.10-25	Ezra 1
Acts 26.1,9-25	Matthew 8.23-34	John 7.14-36
If the Second Service is a Eucharist, the following is read as a Gospel:		
Mark 9.30-37		
Third Service		
Psalm 119.153-176	Psalm 119.153-176	Psalms 130, 131
Isaiah 45.9-22	Isaiah 45.9-22	Isaiah 45.9-22
Revelation 14.1-5	Revelation 14.1-5	Revelation 14.1-5

Proper 21

Sunday between 25 September and 1 October inclusive

YEAR A	YEAR B	YEAR C
Principal Service		
CONTINUOUS	CONTINUOUS	CONTINUOUS
Exodus 17.1-7	Esther 7.1-6,9-10;	Jeremiah 32.1-3a,6-15
Psalm 78.1-4,12-16*	9.20-22	Psalm 91.1-6,14-16*
Philippians 2.1-13	Psalm 124	1 Timothy 6.6-19
Matthew 21.23-32	James 5.13-20	Luke 16.19-31
	Mark 9.38-50	
	or	
RELATED	RELATED	RELATED
Ezekiel 18.1-4,25-32	Numbers 11.4-6,10-	Amos 6.1a,4-7
Psalm 25.1-9	16,24-29	Psalm 146
Philippians 2.1-13	Psalm 19.7-14	1 Timothy 6.6-19
Matthew 21.23-32	James 5.13-20	Luke 16.19-31
	Mark 9.38-50	
Second Service		
Psalms [120, 123] 124	Psalms 120, 121	Psalms 134, 135*
Ezekiel 37.15-28	Exodus 24	Nehemiah 2
1 John 2.22-29	Matthew 9.1-8	John 8.31-38,48-59
If the Second Service is a Eucharist, the following is read as a Gospel:		
Mark 9.38-50		
Third Service		
Psalms 125, 126, 127	Psalm 122	Psalm 132
Isaiah 48.12-21	Isaiah 48.12-22	Isaiah 48.12-22
Luke 11.37-54	Luke 11.37-54	Luke 11.37-54

Proper 22

Sunday between 2 and 8 October inclusive

YEAR A	YEAR B	YEAR C
Principal Service		
CONTINUOUS	CONTINUOUS	CONTINUOUS
Exodus 20.1-4,7-9, 12-20 Psalm 19* Philippians 3.4b-14 Matthew 21.33-46	Job 1.1; 2.1-10 Psalm 26 Hebrews 1.1-4; 2.5-12 Mark 10.2-16	Lamentations 1.1-6 *Canticle:* Lamentations 3.19-26 *or* Psalm 137* 2 Timothy 1.1-14 Luke 17.5-10
	or	
RELATED	RELATED	RELATED
Isaiah 5.1-7 Psalm 80.7-15 Philippians 3.4b-14 Matthew 21.33-46	Genesis 2.18-24 Psalm 8 Hebrews 1.1-4; 2.5-12 Mark 10.2-16	Habakkuk 1.1-4; 2.1-4 Psalm 37.1-9 2 Timothy 1.1-14 Luke 17.5-10
Second Service		
Psalm 136* Proverbs 2.1-11 1 John 2.1-17 If the Second Service is a Eucharist, the following is read as a Gospel: Mark 10.2-16	Psalms 125, 126 Joshua 3.7-17 Matthew 10.1-22	Psalm 142 Nehemiah 5.1-13 John 9
Third Service		
Psalms 128, 129, 134 Isaiah 49.13-23 Luke 12.1-12	Psalms 123, 124 Isaiah 49.13-23 Luke 12.1-12	Psalm 141 Isaiah 49.13-23 Luke 12.1-12

Proper 23

Sunday between 9 and 15 October inclusive

YEAR A	YEAR B	YEAR C
Principal Service		
CONTINUOUS	CONTINUOUS	CONTINUOUS
Exodus 32.1-14	Job 23.1-9,16-17	Jeremiah 29.1,4-7
Psalm 106.1-6,19-23*	Psalm 22.1-15	Psalm 66.1-12
Philippians 4.1-9	Hebrews 4.12-16	2 Timothy 2.8-15
Matthew 22.1-14	Mark 10.17-31	Luke 17.11-19
	or	
RELATED	RELATED	RELATED
Isaiah 25.1-9	Amos 5.6-7,10-15	2 Kings 5.1-3,7-15c
Psalm 23	Psalm 90.12-17	Psalm 111
Philippians 4.1-9	Hebrews 4.12-16	2 Timothy 2.8-15
Matthew 22.1-14	Mark 10.17-31	Luke 17.11-19
Second Service		
Psalm 139.1-18*	Psalms 127 [128]	Psalm 144
Proverbs 3.1-18	Joshua 5.13 – 6.20	Nehemiah 6.1-16
1 John 3.1-15	Matthew 11.20-30	John 15.12-27
If the Second Service is a Eucharist, the following is read as a Gospel:		
Mark 10.17-31		
Third Service		
Psalms 138, 141	Psalms 129, 130	Psalm 143
Isaiah 50.4-10	Isaiah 50.4-10	Isaiah 50.4-10
Luke 13.22-30	Luke 13.22-30	Luke 13.22-30

Proper 24

Sunday between 16 and 22 October inclusive

YEAR A	YEAR B	YEAR C
Principal Service		
CONTINUOUS	CONTINUOUS	CONTINUOUS
Exodus 33.12-23	Job 38.1-7[34-41]	Jeremiah 31.27-34
Psalm 99*	Psalm 104.1-9,24,35c*	Psalm 119.97-104
1 Thessalonians 1.1-10	Hebrews 5.1-10	2 Timothy 3.14 – 4.5
Matthew 22.15-22	Mark 10.35-45	Luke 18.1-8
	or	
RELATED	RELATED	RELATED
Isaiah 45.1-7	Isaiah 53.4-12	Genesis 32.22-31
Psalm 96.1-9[10-13]	Psalm 91.9-16	Psalm 121
1 Thessalonians 1.1-10	Hebrews 5.1-10	2 Timothy 3.14 – 4.5
Matthew 22.15-22	Mark 10.35-45	Luke 18.1-8
Second Service		
Psalms 142 [143.1-11]	Psalm 141	Psalms [146] 149
Proverbs 4.1-18	Joshua 14.6-14	Nehemiah 8.9-18
1 John 3.16 – 4.6	Matthew 12.1-21	John 16.1-11
If the Second Service is a Eucharist, the following is read as a Gospel:		
Mark 10.35-45		
Third Service		
Psalms 145, 149	Psalms 133, 134,	Psalm 147
Isaiah 54.1-14	137.1-6	Isaiah 54.1-14
Luke 13.31-35	Isaiah 54.1-14	Luke 13.31-35
	Luke 13.31-35	

Proper 25

Sunday between 23 and 29 October inclusive

YEAR A	YEAR B	YEAR C
Principal Service		
CONTINUOUS	CONTINUOUS	CONTINUOUS
Deuteronomy 34.1-12	Job 42.1-6,10-17	Joel 2.23-32
Psalm 90.1-6,13-17*	Psalm 34.1-8,19-22*	Psalm 65*
1 Thessalonians 2.1-8	Hebrews 7.23-28	2 Timothy 4.6-8,16-18
Matthew 22.34-46	Mark 10.46-52	Luke 18.9-14
	or	
RELATED	RELATED	RELATED
Leviticus 19.1-2,15-18	Jeremiah 31.7-9	Ecclesiasticus 35.12-17
Psalm 1	Psalm 126	or Jeremiah 14.7-10,
1 Thessalonians 2.1-8	Hebrews 7.23-28	19-22
Matthew 22.34-46	Mark 10.46-52	Psalm 84.1-7
		2 Timothy 4.6-8,16-18
		Luke 18.9-14
Second Service		
Psalms 119.89-104	Psalm 119.121-136	Psalm 119.1-16
Ecclesiastes 11, 12	Ecclesiastes 11, 12	Ecclesiastes 11, 12
2 Timothy 2.1-7	2 Timothy 2.1-7	2 Timothy 2.1-7
If the Second Service is a Eucharist, the following is read as a Gospel:	If the Second Service is a Eucharist, the following is read as a Gospel:	If the Second Service is a Eucharist, the following is read as a Gospel:
Mark 12.28-34	Luke 18.9-14	Matthew 22.34-46
Third Service		
Psalm 119.137-152	Psalm 119.89-104	Psalm 119.105-128
Isaiah 59.9-20	Isaiah 59.9-20	Isaiah 59.9-20
Luke 14.1-14	Luke 14.1-14	Luke 14.1-14

Bible Sunday

YEAR A	YEAR B	YEAR C
Principal Service		
Nehemiah 8.1-4a[5-6] 8-12 Psalm 119.9-16 Colossians 3.12-17 Matthew 24.30-35	Isaiah 55.1-11 Psalm 19.7-14 2 Timothy 3.14 – 4.5 John 5.36b-47	Isaiah 45.22-25 Psalm 119.129-136 Romans 15.1-6 Luke 4.16-24
Second Service		
Psalm 119.89-104 Isaiah 55.1-11 Luke 4.14-30	Psalm 119.1-16 2 Kings 22 Colossians 3.12-17	Psalm 119.1-16 Jeremiah 36.9-32 Romans 10.5-17 If the Second Service is a Eucharist, the following is read as a Gospel: Matthew 22.34-40
Third Service		
Psalm 119.137-152 Deuteronomy 17.14-15,18-20 John 5.36b-47	Psalm 119.89-104 Isaiah 45.22-45 Matthew 24.30-35 *or* Luke 14.1-14	Psalm 119.105-128 1 Kings 22.1-17 Romans 15.4-13 *or* Luke 14.1-14

Dedication Festival

The First Sunday in October or Last Sunday after Trinity

Evening Prayer on the Eve Years A, B, C
Psalm 24 2 Chronicles 7.11-16 John 4.19-29

YEAR A	YEAR B	YEAR C
Principal Service		
1 Kings 8.22-30 *or* Revelation 21.9-14 Psalm 122 Hebrews 12.18-24 Matthew 21.12-16	Genesis 28.11-18 *or* Revelation 21.9-14 Psalm 122 1 Peter 2.1-10 John 10.22-29	1 Chronicles 29.6-19 Psalm 122 Ephesians 2.19-22 John 2.13-22
Second Service		
Psalm 132 Jeremiah 7.1-11 1 Corinthians 3.9-17	Psalm 132 Jeremiah 7.1-11 Luke 19.1-10	Psalm 132 Jeremiah 7.1-11 Luke 19.1-10
Third Service (Readings for Years A, B, C are the same)		
Psalm 48 Haggai 2.6-9 Hebrews 10.19-25	Psalm 48 Haggai 2.6-9 Hebrews 10.19-25	Psalm 48 Haggai 2.6-9 Hebrews 10.19-25

All Saints' Day

Sunday between 30 October and 5 November or, if this is not kept as All Saints' Sunday, on 1 November itself

Evening Prayer on the Eve (if required)
Psalms 1, 5
Ecclesiasticus 44.1-15
or Isaiah 40.27-31
Revelation 19.6-10

YEAR A	YEAR B	YEAR C
Eucharist		
Revelation 7.9-17	Wisdom 3.1-9 *or*	Daniel 7.1-3,15-18
Psalm 34.1-10	Isaiah 25.6-9	Psalm 149
1 John 3.1-3	Psalm 24.1-6	Ephesians 1.11-23
Matthew 5.1-12	Revelation 21.1-6a	Luke 6.20-31
	John 11.32-44	
Morning Prayer		
Psalms 15, 84	Psalms 15, 84	Psalms 15, 84
Isaiah 35.1-9	Isaiah 35.1-9	Isaiah 35.1-9
Luke 9.18-27	Luke 9.18-27	Luke 9.18-27
Evening Prayer		
Psalms 148, 150	Psalms 148, 150	Psalms 148, 150
Isaiah 65.17-25	Isaiah 65.17-25	Isaiah 65.17-25
Hebrews 11.32 – 12.2	Hebrews 11.32 – 12.2	Hebrews 11.32 – 12.2

On 1 November if the material above is used on the Sunday:

Eucharist
Isaiah 56.3-8 *or*
2 Esdras 2.42-48
Psalm 33.1-5
Hebrews 12.18-24
Matthew 5.1-12

Morning Prayer
Psalms 111, 112, 117
Wisdom 5.1-16 *or*
Jeremiah 31.31-34
2 Corinthians 4.5-12

Evening Prayer
Psalm 145
Isaiah 66.20-23
Colossians 1.9-14

The Fourth Sunday Before Advent

Sunday between 30 October and 5 November inclusive
For use if the Feast of All Saints was celebrated on 1 November and
alternative propers are needed

YEAR A	YEAR B	YEAR C
Principal Service		
Micah 3.5-12	Deuteronomy 6.1-9	Isaiah 1.10-18
Psalm 43*	Psalm 119.1-8	Psalm 32.1-7
1 Thessalonians 2.9-13	Hebrews 9.11-14	2 Thessalonians 1.1-12
Matthew 24.1-14	Mark 12.28-34	Luke 19.1-10
Second Service		
Psalms 111, 117	Psalm 145*	Psalm 145*
Daniel 7.1-18	Daniel 2.1-48 (*or* 1-11,	Lamentations 3.22-33
Luke 6.17-31	25-48)	John 11.[1-31]32-44
	Revelation 7.9-17	
	If the Second Service is a Eucharist, the following is read as a Gospel:	
	Matthew 5.1-12	
Third Service		
Psalm 33	Psalms 112, 149	Psalm 87
Isaiah 66.20-23	Jeremiah 31.31-34	Job 19.21-27a
Ephesians 1.11-23	1 John 3.1-3	Colossians 1.9-14

The Third Sunday Before Advent

Sunday between 6 and 12 November inclusive

YEAR A	YEAR B	YEAR C
Principal Service		
Wisdom of Solomon 6.12-16 *Canticle:* Wisdom of Solomon 6.17-20 1 Thessalonians 4.13-18 Matthew 25.1-13 *or* Amos 5.18-24 Psalm 70 1 Thessalonians 4.13-18 Matthew 25.1-13	Jonah 3.1-5,10 Psalm 62.5-12 Hebrews 9.24-28 Mark 1.14-20	Job 19.23-27a Psalm 17.1-9* 2 Thessalonians 2.1-5, 13-17 Luke 20.27-38
Second Service		
Psalms [20] 82 Judges 7.2-22 John 15.9-17	Psalms 46 [82] Isaiah 10.33 – 11.9 John 14.1-29 (*or* 23-29)	Psalm 40 1 Kings 3.1-15 Romans 8.31-39 If the Second Service is a Eucharist, the following is read as a Gospel: Matthew 22.15-22
Third Service		
Psalm 91 Deuteronomy 17.14-20 1 Timothy 2.1-7	Psalm 136 Micah 4.1-5 Philippians 4.6-9	Psalms 20, 90 Isaiah 2.1-5 James 3.13-18

The Second Sunday Before Advent

Sunday between 13 and 19 November inclusive

YEAR A	YEAR B	YEAR C
Principal Service		
Zephaniah 1.7,12-18 Psalm 90.1-8[9-11]12* 1 Thessalonians 5.1-11 Matthew 25.14-30	Daniel 12.1-3 Psalm 16 Hebrews 10.11-14 [15-18]19-25 Mark 13.1-8	Malachi 4.1-2a Psalm 98 2 Thessalonians 3.6-13 Luke 21.5-19
Second Service		
Psalm 89.19-37* 1 Kings 1.15-40 (*or* 1-40) Revelation 1.4-18 <small>If the Second Service is a Eucharist, the following is read as a Gospel:</small> Luke 9.1-6	Psalm 95 Daniel 3 (*or* 3.13-30) Matthew 13.24-30, 36-43	Psalms [93] 97 Daniel 6 Matthew 13.1-9,18-23
Third Service		
Psalm 98 Daniel 10.19-21 Revelation 4	Psalm 96 1 Samuel 9.27 – 10.2a; 10.17-26 Matthew 13.31-35	Psalm 132 1 Samuel 16.1-13 Matthew 13.44-52

Christat the King

Sunday between 20 and 26 November inclusive

Evening Prayer on the Eve Years A, B, C (if required)
Psalms 99, 100 Isaiah 10.33 – 11.9 1 Timothy 6.11-16

YEAR A	YEAR B	YEAR C
Principal Service		
Ezekiel 34.11-16,20-24 Psalm 95.1-7a* Ephesians 1.15-23 Matthew 25.31-46	Daniel 7.9-10,13-14 Psalm 93 Revelation 1.4b-8 John 18.33-37	Jeremiah 23.1-6 Psalm 46 Colossians 1.11-20 Luke 23.33-43
Second Service		
Psalms 93 [97] 2 Samuel 23.1-7 *or* 1 Maccabees 2.15-29 Matthew 28.16-20	Psalm 72* Daniel 5 John 6.1-15	Psalm 72* 1 Samuel 8.4-20 John 18.33-37
Third Service		
Psalms 29, 110 Isaiah 4.2 – 5.7 Luke 19.29-38	Psalms 29, 110 Isaiah 32.1-8 Revelation 3.7-22	Psalms 29, 110 Zechariah 6.9-15 Revelation 11.15-18

Alternative Psalmody for the Principal Service Lectionary

The purpose of this Alternative Psalmody is, in some cases, to reduce the number of verses of a particular provision and, in others, to simplify the reading. Psalms which are starred * have alternatives listed in this table.

	YEAR A	YEAR B	YEAR C
Advent 1		80.1-7	
Advent 2	72.1-7	85.8-13	
Advent 3			146.5-10
Advent 4	80.1-7	89.1-8	
Christmas 1	148.7-14	148.7-14	148.7-14
Epiphany 2		139.1-10	
Epiphany 3	27.1-9		19.1-6
Proper 1		147.1-11	
Proper 3			37.1-7
Lent 1			91.1-11
Lent 3		19.7-14	
Lent 4		107.1-9	
Palm Sunday	118.19-24	118.19-24	118.19-24
	31.9-18	31.9-18	31.9-18
Tuesday in Holy Week	71.1-8	71.1-8	71.1-8
Maundy Thursday	116.11-19	116.11-19	116.11-19
Good Friday	22.1-11 *or* 1-21	22.1-11 *or* 1-21	22.1-11 *or* 1-21
Easter Eve	31.1-5	31.1-5	31.1-5
Easter Day	118.14-24	118.14-24	118.14-24
Easter 3	116.1-8		
Easter 5	31.1-5		148.1-6
Easter 7	68.1-10		
Pentecost	104.24-36	104.24-36	104.24-36
Proper 4	31.19-24		
Proper 6	116.11-18	92.1-8	
Proper 7	86.1-10		42 *or* 43
	69.13-18	107.23-32	
Proper 8	89.8-18		77.11-20
Proper 10	65.9-13		
Proper 11	139.1-12		
Proper 12	105.1-11		85.1-7
Proper 13	17.1-7		107.1-9
	145.14-21		49.1-9
Proper 14	105.1-10		50.1-7
			33.12-21
Proper 15			80.8-19
Proper 17	115	45.1-7	81.1-11
Proper 18			139.1-8
Proper 19	103.8-13	19.1-6	
Proper 20	105.37-45		
Proper 21	78.1-7		91.11-16
Proper 22	19.7-14		137.1-6
Proper 23	106.1-6		
Proper 24	99.1-9	104.1-9	
Proper 25	90.1-6	34.1-8	65.1-8
4 Before Advent	107.1-8		
3 Before Advent			17.1-8
2 Before Advent	90.1-8		
Christ the King	95.1-7		

Alternative Psalmody for the Second Service Lectionary

The purpose of this Alternative Psalmody is to reduce the number of verses of a particular provision. Psalms which are starred * have alternatives listed in this table.

	YEAR A	YEAR B	YEAR C
Advent 1	9.1-8	25.1-10	9.1-8
Advent 2		40.11-17	
Advent 3		68.1-8	
Christmas 2	135.1-14	135.1-14	
Epiphany 3	33.1-12	33.1-12	
Epiphany 4	34.1-10	34.1-10	
2 Before Lent			147.12-20
1 Before Lent			89.5-12
Ash Wednesday	102.1-17	102.1-17	102.1-17
Lent 2	135.1-14	135.1-14	
Lent 5		34.1-10	35.1-9
Wednesday in Holy Week	102.1-17	102.1-17	102.1-17
Easter 7			68.1-14,19-20
Proper 4	33.13-21	35.1-10	
Proper 5			44.1-8
Proper 8	50.1-15		
Proper 10		66.1-9	77.1-12
Proper 11		73.21-28	
Proper 12		74.12-17	88.1-9
Proper 13	80.1-7	88.1-9	107.1-12
Proper 14		91.1-12	
Proper 15	90.1-12		119.17-24
Proper 16		116.12-19	119.49-56
Proper 17		119.9-16	119.81-88
Proper 18		119.49-56	
Proper 19		119.73-80	
Proper 20	119.121-128	119.137-144	
Proper 21			135.1-14
Proper 22	136.1-9		
Proper 23	139.1-11		
4 Before Advent		145.1-9	145.1-9
2 Before Advent	89.19-29		
Christ the King		72.1-7	72.1-7

The Naming and Circumcision of Jesus

1 January

Evening Prayer on the Eve (if required)
Psalm 148 Jeremiah 23.1-6 Colossians 2.8-15

Eucharist	Morning Prayer	Evening Prayer
Numbers 6.22-27 Psalm 8 Galatians 4.4-7 Luke 2.15-21	Psalm 103 Genesis 17.1-13 Romans 2.17-29	Psalm 115 Deuteronomy 30.[1-10]11-20 Acts 3.1-16

The Conversion of Paul

25 January

Evening Prayer on the Eve (if required)
Psalm 149 Isaiah 49.1-13 Acts 22.3-16

Eucharist	Morning Prayer	Evening Prayer
Jeremiah 1.4-10 Psalm 67 Acts 9.1-22 Matthew 19.27-30 or Acts 9.1-22 Psalm 67 Galatians 1.11-16a Matthew 19.27-30	Psalm 66 Ezekiel 3.22-27 Philippians 3.1-14	Psalm 119.41-56 Ecclesiasticus 39.1-10 or Isaiah 56.1-8 Colossians 1.24 – 2.7

Timothy and Titus

26 January   *Lesser Festival*

Eucharist
Isaiah 61.1-3a
Psalm 100
2 Timothy 2.1-8 *or*
Titus 1.1-5
Luke 10.1-9

Joseph

19 March

Evening Prayer on the Eve (if required)
Psalm 132
Hosea 11.1-9
Luke 2.41-52

Eucharist	Morning Prayer	Evening Prayer
2 Samuel 7.4-16	Psalm 25	Psalms 1, 112
Psalm 89.27-36	Isaiah 11.1-10	Genesis 50.22-26
Romans 4.13-18	Matthew 13.54-58	Matthew 2.13-23
Matthew 1.18-25		

The Annunciation

25 March   *Principal Feast*

Evening Prayer on the Eve
Psalm 85
Wisdom 9.1-12 *or*
Genesis 3.8-15
Galatians 4.1-5

Eucharist	Morning Prayer	Evening Prayer
Isaiah 7.10-14	Psalms 111, 113	Psalms 131, 146
Psalm 40.5-10	1 Samuel 2.1-10	Isaiah 52.1-12
Hebrews 10.4-10	Romans 5.12-21	Hebrews 2.5-18
Luke 1.26-38		

George

23 April

Evening Prayer on the Eve (if required)
Psalms 111, 116 Jeremiah 15.15-21 Hebrews 11.32 – 12.2

Eucharist	Morning Prayer	Evening Prayer
1 Maccabees 2.59-64 *or* Revelation 12.7-12 Psalm 126 2 Timothy 2.3-13 John 15.18-21	Psalm 5 Joshua 1.1-9 Ephesians 6.10-20	Psalms 3, 11 Isaiah 43.1-7 John 15.1-8

Mark

25 April

Evening Prayer on the Eve (if required)
Psalm 19 Isaiah 52.7-10 Mark 1.1-15

Eucharist	Morning Prayer	Evening Prayer

Proverbs 15.28-33 *or*
  Acts 15.35-41
Psalm 119.9-16
Ephesians 4.7-16
Mark 13.5-13
	Psalm 37.23-40
	Isaiah 62.6-10 *or*
	  Ecclesiasticus 51.13-
	  30
	Acts 12.25 – 13.13
		Psalm 45
		Ezekiel 1.4-14
		2 Timothy 4.1-11

Philip and James

1 May

Evening Prayer on the Eve (if required)
Psalm 25 Isaiah 40.27-31 John 12.20-26

Eucharist	Morning Prayer	Evening Prayer
Isaiah 30.15-21 Psalm 119.1-8 Ephesians 1.3-10 John 14.1-14	Psalm 139 Proverbs 4.10-18 James 1.1-12	Psalm 149 Job 23.1-12 John 1.43-51

English Saints of the Reformation Era

4 May   *Lesser Festival*

Eucharist
Isaiah 43.1-7 *or*
Ecclesiasticus 2.10-17
Psalm 87
2 Corinthians 4.5-12
John 12.20-26

Matthias

14 May

Evening Prayer on the Eve (if required)
Psalm 147
Isaiah 22.15-22
Philippians 3.13b – 4.1

Eucharist	Morning Prayer	Evening Prayer
Isaiah 22.15-25	Psalm 16	Psalm 80
Psalm 15	1 Samuel 2.27-35	1 Samuel 16.1-13a
Acts 1.15-26	Acts 2.37-47	Matthew 7.15-27
John 15.9-17		
or		
Acts 1.15-26		
Psalm 15		
1 Corinthians 4.1-7		
John 15.9-17		

The Visit of Mary to Elizabeth

31 May

Evening Prayer on the Eve (if required)
Psalm 45
Song of Solomon 2.8-14
Luke 1.26-38

Eucharist	Morning Prayer	Evening Prayer
Zephaniah 3.14-18	Psalm 85	Psalms 122, 127, 128
Psalm 113	1 Samuel 2.1-10	Zechariah 2.10-13
Romans 12.9-16	Mark 3.31-35	John 3.25-30
Luke 1.39-49[50-56]		

Barnabas

11 June

Eucharist	Morning Prayer	Evening Prayer
Job 29.11-16	Psalms 100, 101	Psalm 147
Psalm 112	Jeremiah 9.23-24	Ecclesiastes 12.9-14 or
Acts 11.19-30	Acts 4.32-37	Tobit 4.5-11
John 15.12-17		Acts 9.26-31
or		
Acts 11.19-30		
Psalm 112		
Galatians 2.1-10		
John 15.12-17		

The Birth of John the Baptist

24 June

Evening Prayer on the Eve (if required)
Psalm 71
Judges 13.2-7,24-25
Luke 1.5-25

Eucharist	Morning Prayer	Evening Prayer
Isaiah 40.1-11	Psalm 50	Psalms 80, 82
Psalm 85.7-13	Ecclesiasticus 48.1-10	Malachi 4
Acts 13.14b-26 or	or Malachi 3.1-6	Matthew 11.2-19
Galatians 3.23-29	Luke 3.1-17	
Luke 1.57-66,80		

Peter and Paul

29 June

Evening Prayer on the Eve (if required)
Psalms 66, 67
Ezekiel 3.4-11
Galatians 1.13 – 2.8

Eucharist	Morning Prayer	Evening Prayer
Zechariah 4.1-6a,10b-14	Psalm 71	Psalms 124, 138
Psalm 125	Isaiah 49.1-6	Ezekiel 34.11-16
Acts 12.1-11	Acts 11.1-18	John 21.15-22
Matthew 16.13-19		
or		
Acts 12.1-11		
Psalm 125		
2 Timothy 4.6-8,17-18		
Matthew 16.13-19		

or for Peter *alone*

29 June

Evening Prayer on the Eve (if required)
Psalms 66, 67
Ezekiel 3.4-11
Acts 9.32-43

Eucharist	Morning Prayer	Evening Prayer
Ezekiel 3.22-27	Psalm 71	Psalms 124, 138
Psalm 125	Isaiah 49.1-6	Ezekiel 34.11-16
Acts 12.1-11	Acts 11.1-18	John 21.15-22
Matthew 16.13-19		
or		
Acts 12.1-11		
Psalm 125		
1 Peter 2.19-25		
Matthew 16.13-19		

Thomas

3 July

Eucharist	Morning Prayer	Evening Prayer
Habakkuk 2.1-4	Psalms 92, 146	Psalm 139
Psalm 31.1-6	2 Samuel 15.17-21 *or*	Job 42.1-6
Ephesians 2.19-22	Ecclesiasticus 2	1 Peter 1.3-12
John 20.24-29	John 11.1-16	

Mary Magdalene

22 July

Evening Prayer on the Eve (if required)
Psalm 139
Isaiah 25.1-9
2 Corinthians 1.3-7

Eucharist	Morning Prayer	Evening Prayer
Song of Solomon 3.1-4	Psalms 30, 32	Psalm 63
Psalm 42.1-7	1 Samuel 16.14-23	Zephaniah 3.14-20
2 Corinthians 5.14-17	Luke 8.1-3	Mark 15.40 – 16.7
John 20.1-2,11-18		

James

25 July

Psalm 144
Deuteronomy 30.11-20
Mark 5.21-43

Eucharist	Morning Prayer	Evening Prayer
Jeremiah 45.1-5 Psalm 126 Acts 11.27 – 12.2 Matthew 20.20-28 or Acts 11.27 – 12.2 Psalm 126 2 Corinthians 4.7-15 Matthew 20.20-28	Psalms 7, 29 2 Kings 1.9-15 Luke 9.46-56	Psalm 94 Jeremiah 26.1-15 Mark 1.14-20

Anne and Joachim

26 July   *Lesser Festival*

Eucharist
Zephaniah 4.14-17 Psalm 127 Romans 8.28-30 Matthew 13.16-17

Mary, Martha and Lazarus

29 July   *Lesser Festival*

Eucharist
Isaiah 25.6-9 Psalm 49.5-10,16 Hebrews 2.10-15 John 12.1-8

The Transfiguration

6 August

Evening Prayer on the Eve (if required)
Psalms 99, 110
Exodus 24.12-18
John 12.27-36a

Eucharist	Morning Prayer	Evening Prayer
Daniel 7.9-10,13-14	Psalm 27	Psalm 72
Psalm 97	Ecclesiasticus 48.1-10	Exodus 34.29-35
2 Peter 1.16-19	or 1 Kings 19.1-16	2 Corinthians 3
Luke 9.28-36	1 John 3.1-3	

The Blessed Virgin Mary

15 August

Evening Prayer on the Eve (if required)
Psalm 72
Proverbs 8.22-31
John 19.23-27

Eucharist	Morning Prayer	Evening Prayer
Isaiah 61.10,11 or	Psalms 98, 138	Psalm 132
Revelation 11.19 –	Isaiah 7.10-15	Song of Solomon 2.1-7
12.6,10	Luke 11.27-28	Acts 1.6-14
Psalm 45.10-17		
Galatians 4.4-7		
Luke 1.46-55		

Bartholomew

24 August

Evening Prayer on the Eve (if required)
Psalm 97
Isaiah 61.1-9
2 Corinthians 6.1-10

Eucharist	Morning Prayer	Evening Prayer
Isaiah 43.8-13	Psalm 86	Psalms 91, 116
Psalm 145.1-7	Genesis 28.10-17	Ecclesiasticus 39.1-10
Acts 5.12-16	John 1.43-51	*or* Deuteronomy
Luke 22.24-30		18.15-19
		Matthew 10.1-22
or		
Acts 5.12-16		
Psalm 145.1-7		
1 Corinthians 4.9-15		
Luke 22.24-30		

The Beheading of John the Baptist

29 August   *Lesser Festival*

Eucharist
Jeremiah 1.4-10
Psalm 11
Hebrews 11.32 – 12.2
Matthew 14.1-12

Holy Cross Day

14 September

Evening Prayer on the Eve (if required)
Psalm 66
Isaiah 52.13 – 53.12
Ephesians 2.11-22

Eucharist	Morning Prayer	Evening Prayer
Numbers 21.4-9	Psalms 2, 8	Psalms 110, 150
Psalm 22.23-28	Genesis 3.1-15	Isaiah 63.1-16
Philippians 2.6-11	John 12.27-36a	1 Corinthians 1.18-25
John 3.13-17		

Matthew

21 September

Evening Prayer on the Eve (if required)
Psalm 34 Isaiah 33.13-17 Matthew 6.19-34

Eucharist	Morning Prayer	Evening Prayer
Proverbs 3.13-18 Psalm 119.65-72 2 Corinthians 4.1-6 Matthew 9.9-13	Psalm 49 1 Kings 19.15-21 2 Timothy 3.14-17	Psalm 119.33-40,89-96 Ecclesiastes 5.4-12 Matthew 19.16-30

Michael and All Angels

29 September

Evening Prayer on the Eve (if required)
Psalm 91 2 Kings 6.8-17 Matthew 18.1-6,10

Eucharist	Morning Prayer	Evening Prayer
Genesis 28.10-17 Psalm 103.19-22 Revelation 12.7-12 John 1.47-51 or Revelation 12.7-12 Psalm 103.19-22 Hebrews 1.5-14 John 1.47-51	Psalm 34 Tobit 12.6-22 or Daniel 12.1-4 Acts 12.1-11	Psalms 138, 148 Daniel 10.4-21 Revelation 5

Luke

18 October

Eucharist	Morning Prayer	Evening Prayer
Isaiah 35.3-6 *or* Acts 16.6-12a Psalm 147.1-7 2 Timothy 4.5-17 Luke 10.1-9	Psalm 145 Isaiah 55 Luke 1.1-4	Psalm 103 Ecclesiasticus 38.1-14 *or* Isaiah 61.1-6 Colossians 4.7-18

Simon and Jude

28 October

Evening Prayer on the Eve (if required)
Psalms 124, 125, 126
Deuteronomy 32.1-4
John 14.15-26

Eucharist	Morning Prayer	Evening Prayer
Isaiah 28.14-16 Psalm 119.89-96 Ephesians 2.19-22 John 15.17-27	Psalm 116 Wisdom 5.1-16 *or* Isaiah 45.18-26 Luke 6.12-16	Psalm 119.1-16 1 Maccabees 2.42-66 *or* Jeremiah 3.11-18 Jude 1-4,17-25

Commemoration of the Faithful Departed (All Souls' Day)

2 November   *Lesser Festival*

Eucharist
Lamentations 3.17-26, 31-33 *or* Wisdom 3.1-9 Psalm 23 *or* 27.1-6,16-17 Romans 5.5-11 *or* 1 Peter 1.3-9 John 5.19-25 *or* John 6.37-40

Saints and Martyrs of England

8 November

Eucharist
Isaiah 61.4-9 *or* Ecclesiasticus 44.1-15 Psalm 15 Revelation 19.5-10 John 17.18-23

Andrew

30 November

Evening Prayer on the Eve (if required)
Psalm 48 Isaiah 49.1-9a 1 Corinthians 4.9-16

Eucharist	Morning Prayer	Evening Prayer
Isaiah 52.7-10 Psalm 19.1-6 Romans 10.12-18 Matthew 4.18-22	Psalms 46, 47 Ezekiel 47.1-12 *or* Ecclesiasticus 14.20-27 John 12.20-32	Psalms 87, 96 Zechariah 8.20-23 John 1.35-42

Stephen

26 December

Eucharist	Morning Prayer	Evening Prayer
2 Chronicles 24.20-22 Psalm 119.161-168 Acts 7.51-60 Matthew 23.34-39 *or* Acts 7.51-60 Psalm 119.161-168 Galatians 2.16b-20 Matthew 23.34-39	Psalms 13; 31.1-8 Jeremiah 26.12-15 Acts 6	Psalms 57, 86 Genesis 4.1-10 Matthew 10.17-22

John

27 December

Eucharist	Morning Prayer	Evening Prayer
Exodus 33.7-11a Psalm 117 1 John 1 John 21.19b-25	Psalm 21 Exodus 33.7-11a 1 John 2.1-11	Psalm 97 Isaiah 6.1-8 1 John 5.1-12

Holy Innocents

28 December

Eucharist	Morning Prayer	Evening Prayer
Jeremiah 31.15-17 Psalm 124 1 Corinthians 1.26-29 Matthew 2.8-13	Psalms 8, 36 Baruch 4.21-27 *or* Genesis 37.13-20 Matthew 18.1-10	Psalms 123, 128 Isaiah 49.14-25 Mark 10.13-16

Common of the Saints

The Blessed Virgin Mary

Genesis 3.8-15,20; Isaiah 7.10-14; Micah 5.1-4

Acts 1.12-14; Romans 8.18-30; Galatians 4.4-7

Psalms 45.10-17; 113; 131

Luke 1.26-38; Luke 1.39-47; John 19.25-27

Martyrs

2 Chronicles 24.17-21; Isaiah 43.1-7; Jeremiah 11.18-20; Wisdom 4.10-15

Romans 8.35-39; 2 Corinthians 4.7-15; 2 Timothy 2.3-7[8-13]; Hebrews 11.32-40; 1 Peter 4.12-19; Revelation 12.10-12a

Psalms 3; 11; 31.1-5; 44.18-23; 126

Matthew 10.16-22; Matthew 10.28-39; Matthew 16.24-26; John 12.24-26; John 15.18-21

> For Agnes: also Revelation 7.13-17
> For Charles: also Ecclesiasticus 2.12-17; 1 Timothy 6.12-16
> For Janani Luwum: also Ecclesiasticus 4.20-28; John 12.24-32
> For Polycarp: also Revelation 2.8-11
> For Perpetua: especially Revelation 12.10-12a; also Wisdom 3.1-7
> For Alphege: also Hebrews 5.1-4
> For Justin: especially John 15.18-21; also 1 Maccabees 2.15-22;
>   1 Corinthians 1.18-25
> For Boniface: also Acts 20.24-28
> For Alban: especially 2 Timothy 2.3-13; John 12.24-26
> For Oswald: especially 1 Peter 4.12-19; John 16.29-33
> For Laurence: also 2 Corinthians 9.6-10
> For Cyprian: especially 1 Peter 4.12-19; also Matthew 18.18-22
> For John Coleridge Patteson: especially 2 Chronicles 24.17-21; also Acts
>   7.55-60
> For William Tyndale: also Proverbs 8.4-11; 2 Timothy 3.12-17
> For Ignatius: also Philippians 3.7-12; John 6.52-58
> For James Hannington: especially Matthew 10.28-39
> For Edmund: also Proverbs 20.28; 21.1-4,7
> For Clement: also Philippians 3.17 – 4.3; Matthew 16.13-19
> For Lucy: also Wisdom 3.1-7; 2 Corinthians 4.6-15
> For Thomas Becket: especially Matthew 10.28-33; also Ecclesiasticus 51.1-8

Teachers of the Faith and Spiritual Writers

1 Kings 3.[6-10]11-14; Proverbs 4.1-9; Wisdom 7.7-10,15-16; Ecclesiasticus 39.1-10

1 Corinthians 1.18-25; 1 Corinthians 2.1-10; 1 Corinthians 2.9-16; Ephesians 3.8-12; 2 Timothy 4.1-8; Titus 2.1-8

Psalms 19.7-10; 34.11-17; 37.30-35; 119.85-96; 119.97-104

Matthew 5.13-19; Matthew 13.52-58; Matthew 23.8-12; Mark 4.1-9; John 16.12-15

> *For Basil and Gregory: especially 2 Timothy 4.1-8; Matthew 5.13-19*
> *For Hilary: also 1 John 2.18-25; John 8.25-32*
> *For Francis de Sales: also Proverbs 3.13-18; John 3.17-21*
> *For Thomas Aquinas: especially Wisdom 7.7-10,15-16; 1 Corinthians 2.9-16; John 16.12-15*
> *For William Law: especially 1 Corinthians 2.9-16; also Matthew 17.1-9*
> *For Anselm: also Wisdom 9.13-18; Romans 5.8-11*
> *For Catherine of Siena: also Proverbs 8.1,6-11; John 17.12-26*
> *For Athanasius: also Ecclesiasticus 4.20-28; also Matthew 10.24-27*
> *For Irenæus: also 2 Peter 1.16-21*
> *For Gregory and Macrina of Nyssa: especially 1 Corinthians 2.9-13; also Wisdom 9.13-17*
> *For Jeremy Taylor: also Titus 2.7-8,11-14*
> *For Bernard: especially Revelation 19.5-9*
> *For Augustine of Hippo: especially Ecclesiasticus 39.1-10; also Romans 13.11-13*
> *For John Bunyan: also Hebrews 12.1-2; Luke 21.21,34-36*
> *For Gregory the Great: also 1 Thessalonians 2.3-8*
> *For John Chrysostom: especially Matthew 5.13-19; also Jeremiah 1.4-10*
> *For Teresa of Avila: also Romans 8.22-27*
> *For Richard Hooker: especially John 16.12-15; also Ecclesiasticus 44.10-15*
> *For Leo: also 1 Peter 5.1-11*
> *For Ambrose: also Isaiah 41.9b-13; Luke 22.24-30*
> *For John of the Cross: especially 1 Corinthians 2.1-10; also John 14.18-23*

Bishops and Other Pastors

1 Samuel 16.1,6-13; Isaiah 6.1-8; Jeremiah 1.4-10; Ezekiel 3.16-21; Malachi 2.5-7

Acts 20.28-35; 1 Corinthians 4.1-5; 2 Corinthians 4.1-10 (*or* 1,2,5-7); 2 Corinthians 5.14-20; 1 Peter 5.1-4

Psalms 1; 15; 16.5-11; 96; 110

Matthew 11.25-30; Matthew 24.42-46; John 10.11-16; John 15.9-17; John 21.15-17

> *For Wulfstan: especially Matthew 24.42-46*
> *For George Herbert: especially Malachi 2.5-7; Matthew 11.25-30; also Revelation 19.5-9*
> *For David: also 2 Samuel 23.1-4; Psalm 89.19-23,25*
> *For Edward King: also Hebrews 13.1-8*
> *For Dunstan: especially Matthew 24.42-46: also Exodus 31.1-5*
> *For John and Charles Wesley: also Ephesians 5.15-20*
> *For Augustine of Canterbury: also 1 Thessalonians 2.2b-8; Matthew 13.31-33*
> *For Thomas Ken: especially 2 Corinthians 4.1-10; Matthew 24.42-46*
> *For Richard: also John 21.15-19*
> *For John Keble: also Lamentations 3.19-26; Matthew 5.1-8*
> *For Swithun: also James 5.7-11,13-18*
> *For Lancelot Andrewes: especially Isaiah 6.1-8*

For Martin of Tours: also 1 Thessalonians 5.1-11; Matthew 25.34-40
For Charles Simeon: especially Malachi 2.5-7; also Colossians 1.3-8;
   Luke 8.4-8
For Hugh: also 1 Timothy 6.11-16
For Nicholas: also Isaiah 61.1-3; 1 Timothy 6.6-11; Mark 10.13-16

Members of Religious Communities

1 Kings 19.9-18; Proverbs 10.27-32; Song of Solomon 8.6-7; Isaiah 61.10 –
62.5; Hosea 2.14-15,19-20

Acts 4.32-35; 2 Corinthians 10.17 – 11.2; Philippians 3.7-14; 1 John 2.15-
17; Revelation 19.1,5-9

Psalms 34.1-8; 112.1-9; 119.57-64; 123; 131

Matthew 11.25-30; Matthew 19.3-12; Matthew 19.23-30; Luke 9.57-62;
Luke 12.32-37
   For Aelred: also Ecclesiasticus 15.1-6
   For Antony: especially Philippians 3.7-14, also Matthew 19.16-26
   For Julian of Norwich: also 1 Corinthians 13.8-13; Matthew 5.13-16
   For Alcuin: also Colossians 3.12-16; John 4.19-24
   For Bede: also Ecclesiasticus 39.1-10
   For Etheldreda: also Matthew 25.1-13
   For Benedict: also 1 Corinthians 3.10,11; Luke 18.18-22
   For Dominic: also Ecclesiasticus 39.1-10
   For Clare: especially Song of Solomon 8.6-7
   For Hildegard: also 1 Corinthians 2.9-13; Luke 10.21-24
   For Vincent de Paul: also 1 Corinthians 1.25-31; Matthew 25.34-40
   For Francis of Assisi: also Galatians 6.14-18; Luke 12.22-34
   For Hilda: especially Isaiah 61.10 – 62.5

Missionaries

Isaiah 52.7-10; Isaiah 61.1-3a; Ezekiel 34.11-16; Jonah 3.1-5

Acts 2.14,22-36; Acts 13.46-49; Acts 16.6-10; Acts 26.19-23; Romans 15.17-
21; 2 Corinthians 5.11 – 6.2

Psalms 67; 87; 97; 100; 117

Matthew 9.35-38; Matthew 28.16-20; Mark 16.15-20; Luke 5.1-11; Luke
10.1-9
   For Anskar: especially Isaiah 52.7-10; also Romans 10.11-15
   For Cyril and Methodius: especially Isaiah 52.7-10; also Romans 10.11-15
   For Chad: also 1 Timothy 6.11b-16
   For Patrick: also Psalm 91.1-4,13-16; Luke 10.1-12,17-20
   For Cuthbert: especially Ezekiel 34.11-16; also Matthew 18.12-14
   For Columba: also Titus 2.11-15
   For Aidan: also 1 Corinthians 9.16-19
   For Ninian: especially Acts 13.46-49; Mark 16.15-20
   For Paulinus: especially Matthew 28.16-20
   For Wilfrid: especially Luke 1.5-11; also 1 Corinthians 1.18-25
   For Henry Martyn: especially Mark 16.15-20; also Isaiah 55.6-11
   For Willibrord: especially Isaiah 52.7-10; Matthew 28.16-20

Any Saint

General
Genesis 12.1-4; Proverbs 8.1-11; Micah 6.6-8; Ecclesiasticus 2.7-13[14-17]

Ephesians 3.14-19; Ephesians 6.11-18; Hebrews 13.7-8,15-16; James 2.14-17; 1 John 4.7-16; Revelation 21.[1-4]5-7

Psalms 32; 33.1-5; 119.1-8; 139.1-5[6-13]; 145.8-13

Matthew 19.16-21; Matthew 25.1-13; Matthew 25.14-30; John 15.1-8; John 17.20-26

Christian rulers
1 Samuel 16.1-13a; 1 Kings 3.3-14

1 Timothy 2.1-6

Psalms 72.1-7; 99

Mark 10.42-45; Luke 14.27-33
> *For Edward the Confessor: also 2 Samuel 23.1-5; 1 John 4.13-16*
> *For Alfred the Great: also 2 Samuel 23.1-5; John 18.33-37*
> *For Margaret of Scotland: also Proverbs 31.10-12,20,26-31; 1 Corinthians 12.13 – 13.3; Matthew 25.34-46*

Those working for the poor and underprivileged
Isaiah 58.6-11

Hebrews 13.1-3; 1 John 3.14-18

Psalms 82; 146.5-12

Matthew 5.1-12; Matthew 25.31-46
> *For Josephine Butler: especially Isaiah 58.6-11; also 1 John 3.18-23; Matthew 9.10-13*
> *For William Wilberforce: also Job 31.16-23; Galatians 3.26-29; 4.6-7; Luke 4.16-21*
> *For Elizabeth of Hungary: especially Matthew 25.31-46; also Proverbs 31.10-31*

Men and women of learning
Proverbs 8.22-31; Ecclesiasticus 44.1-15

Philippians 4.7-8

Psalms 36.5-10; 49.1-4

Matthew 13.44-46,52; John 7.14-18

Those whose holiness was revealed in marriage and family life
Proverbs 31.10-31 (*or* 10-13,19-20,30-31); Tobit 8.4-7

1 Peter 3.1-9

Psalms 127; 128

Mark 3.31-35; Luke 10.38-42
> *For Mary Sumner: also Hebrews 13.1-5*
> *For Monica: also Ecclesiasticus 26.1-3,13-16*

Special Occasions

The Guidance of the Holy Spirit

Proverbs 24.3-7; Isaiah 30.15-21; Wisdom 9.13-17
Acts 15.23-29; Romans 8.22-27; 1 Corinthians 12.4-13
Psalms 25.1-9; 104.26-33; 143.8-10
Luke 14.27-33; John 14.23-26; John 16.13-15

Rogation Days

Deuteronomy 8.1-10; 1 Kings 8.35-40; Job 28.1-11
Philippians 4.4-7; 2 Thessalonians 3.6-13; 1 John 5.12-15
Psalms 104.21-30; 107.1-9; 121
Matthew 6.1-15; Mark 11.22-24; Luke 11.5-13

Harvest Thanksgiving

Year A
Deuteronomy 8.7-18 *or* Deuteronomy 28.1-14
Psalm 65
2 Corinthians 9.6-15
Luke 12.16-30 *or* Luke 17.11-19

Year B
Joel 2.21-27
Psalm 126
1 Timothy 2.1-7 *or* 1 Timothy 6.6-10
Matthew 6.25-33

Year C
Deuteronomy 26.1-11
Psalm 100
Philippians 4.4-9 *or* Revelation 14.14-18
John 6.25-35

Mission and Evangelism

Isaiah 49.1-6; Isaiah 52.7-10; Micah 4.1-5
Acts 17.12-34; 2 Corinthians 5.14 – 6.2; Ephesians 2.13-22
Psalms 2; 46; 67
Matthew 5.13-16; Matthew 28.16-20; John 17.20-26

The Unity of the Church

Jeremiah 33.6-9a; Ezekiel 36.23-28; Zephaniah 3.16-20
Ephesians 4.1-6; Colossians 3.9-17; 1 John 4.9-15
Psalms 100; 122; 133
Matthew 18.19-22; John 11.45-52; John 17.11b-23

The Peace of the World

Isaiah 9.1-6; Isaiah 57.15-19; Micah 4.1-5
Philippians 4.6-9; 1 Timothy 2.1-6; James 3.13-18
Psalms 40.14-17; 72.1-7; 85.8-13
Matthew 5.43-48; John 14.23-29; John 15.9-17

Social Justice and Responsibility

Isaiah 32.15-20; Amos 5.21-24; Amos 8.4-7; Acts 5.1-11
Colossians 3.12-15; James 2.1-4
Psalms 31.21-24; 85.1-7; 146.5-10
Matthew 5.1-12; Matthew 25.31-46; Luke 16.19-31

Ministry (including Ember Days)

Numbers 11.16-17,24-29; Numbers 27.15-23; 1 Samuel 16.1-13a;
Isaiah 6.1-8; Isaiah 61.1-3; Jeremiah 1.4-10
Acts 20.28-35; 1 Corinthians 3.3-11; Ephesians 4.4-16; Philippians 3.7-14
Psalms 40.8-13; 84.8-12; 89.19-25; 101.1-5,7; 122
Luke 4.16-21; Luke 12.35-43; Luke 22.24-27; John 4.31-38; John 15.5-17

In Time of Trouble

Genesis 9.8-17; Job 1.13-22; Isaiah 38.6-11
Romans 3.21-26; Romans 8.18-25; 2 Corinthians 8.1-5,9
Psalms 86.1-7; 107.4-15; 142.1-7
Mark 4.35-41; Luke 12.1-7; John 16.31-33

For the Sovereign

Joshua 1.1-9; Proverbs 8.1-16
Romans 13.1-10; Revelation 21.22 – 22.4
Psalms 20; 101; 121
Matthew 22.16-22; Luke 22.24-30

COLLECTS AND POST COMMUNION PRAYERS

A † symbol beside the word *Collect* or *Post Communion* indicates that a traditional form of this prayer exists in *The Book of Common Prayer*, and that the traditional form may be used in place of the text provided here.

Where a collect ends 'Through Jesus Christ ... now and for ever', the minister may use the shorter ending, 'Through Jesus Christ our Lord' to which the people respond 'Amen' and omit the longer Trinitarian ending. The longer ending is to be preferred at Holy Communion.

The Collect for each Sunday is used on the following weekdays, except where other provision is made.

The First Sunday of Advent

Collect[†]

Almighty God,
give us grace to cast away the works of darkness
and to put on the armour of light,
now in the time of this mortal life,
in which your Son Jesus Christ
   came to us in great humility;
that on the last day,
when he shall come again in his glorious majesty
   to judge the living and the dead,
we may rise to the life immortal;
through him who is alive and reigns with you,
in the unity of the Holy Spirit,
one God, now and for ever.

This Collect may be used as the Post Communion on any day from the Second Sunday of Advent until Christmas Eve instead of the Post Communion provided.

Post Communion

O Lord our God,
make us watchful and keep us faithful
as we await the coming of your Son our Lord;
that, when he shall appear,
he may not find us sleeping in sin
but active in his service
and joyful in his praise;
through Jesus Christ our Lord.

The Second Sunday of Advent

Purple

Collect[†]

O Lord, raise up, we pray, your power
and come among us,
and with great might succour us;
that whereas, through our sins and wickedness
we are grievously hindered
in running the race that is set before us,
your bountiful grace and mercy
may speedily help and deliver us;
through Jesus Christ your Son our Lord,
to whom with you and the Holy Spirit,
be honour and glory, now and for ever.

Post Communion

Father in heaven,
who sent your Son to redeem the world
and will send him again to be our judge:
give us grace so to imitate him
    in the humility and purity of his first coming
that, when he comes again,
we may be ready to greet him
with joyful love and firm faith;
through Jesus Christ our Lord.

The Third Sunday of Advent

Purple

Collect[†]

O Lord Jesus Christ,
who at your first coming sent your messenger
to prepare your way before you:
grant that the ministers and stewards of your mysteries
may likewise so prepare and make ready your way
by turning the hearts of the disobedient
    to the wisdom of the just,
that at your second coming to judge the world
we may be found an acceptable people in your sight;
for you are alive and reign with the Father
in the unity of the Holy Spirit,
one God, now and for ever.

Post Communion

We give you thanks, O Lord, for these heavenly gifts;
kindle in us the fire of your Spirit
that when your Christ comes again
we may shine as lights before his face;
who is alive and reigns now and for ever.

The Fourth Sunday of Advent

Collect

God our redeemer,
who prepared the Blessed Virgin Mary
to be the mother of your Son:
grant that, as she looked for his coming as our saviour,
so we may be ready to greet him
when he comes again as our judge;
who is alive and reigns with you,
in the unity of the Holy Spirit,
one God, now and for ever.

Post Communion

Heavenly Father,
who chose the Blessed Virgin Mary
to be the mother of the promised saviour:
fill us your servants with your grace,
that in all things we may embrace your holy will
and with her rejoice in your salvation;
through Jesus Christ our Lord.

Christmas Eve

24 December *Purple*

Collect

Almighty God,
you make us glad with the yearly remembrance
    of the birth of your Son Jesus Christ:
grant that, as we joyfully receive him as our redeemer,
so we may with sure confidence behold him
when he shall come to be our judge;
who is alive and reigns with you,
in the unity of the Holy Spirit,
one God, now and for ever.

Post Communion

Eternal God, for whom we wait,
you have fed us with the bread of eternal life:
keep us ever watchful,
that we may be ready to stand before the Son of Man,
Jesus Christ our Lord.

Christmas Night

25 December *Gold or White*

Collect
Eternal God,
who made this most holy night
to shine with the brightness of your one true light:
bring us, who have known the revelation
    of that light on earth,
to see the radiance of your heavenly glory;
through Jesus Christ your Son our Lord,
who is alive and reigns with you,
in the unity of the Holy Spirit,
one God, now and for ever.

Post Communion
God our Father,
in this night you have made known to us again
the coming of our Lord Jesus Christ:
confirm our faith and fix our eyes on him
until the day dawns
and Christ the Morning Star rises in our hearts.
To him be glory both now and for ever.

Christmas Day

25 December *Gold or White*

Collect†
Almighty God,
you have given us your only-begotten Son
to take our nature upon him
and as at this time to be born of a pure virgin:
grant that we, who have been born again
and made your children by adoption and grace,
may daily be renewed by your Holy Spirit;
through Jesus Christ your Son our Lord,
who is alive and reigns with you,
in the unity of the Holy Spirit,
one God, now and for ever.

Post Communion
God our Father,
whose Word has come among us
in the Holy Child of Bethlehem:
may the light of faith illumine our hearts
    and shine in our words and deeds;
through him who is Christ the Lord.

The First Sunday of Christmas

White

Collect

Almighty God,
who wonderfully created us in your own image
and yet more wonderfully restored us
through your Son Jesus Christ:
grant that, as he came to share in our humanity,
so we may share the life of his divinity;
who is alive and reigns with you,
in the unity of the Holy Spirit,
one God, now and for ever.

Post Communion

Heavenly Father,
whose blessed Son shared at Nazareth
   the life of an earthly home:
help your Church to live as one family,
united in love and obedience,
and bring us all at last to our home in heaven;
through Jesus Christ our Lord.

The Second Sunday of Christmas

White

Collect

Almighty God,
in the birth of your Son
you have poured on us the new light of your incarnate Word,
and shown us the fullness of your love:
help us to walk in his light and dwell in his love
that we may know the fullness of his joy;
who is alive and reigns with you,
in the unity of the Holy Spirit,
one God, now and for ever.

Post Communion

All praise to you,
almighty God and heavenly King,
who sent your Son into the world
to take our nature upon him
and to be born of a pure virgin:
grant that, as we are born again in him,
so he may continually dwell in us
and reign on earth as he reigns in heaven,
now and for ever.

The Epiphany

6 January   *Gold or White*

Collect[†]

O God,
who by the leading of a star
manifested your only Son to the peoples of the earth:
mercifully grant that we,
who know you now by faith,
may at last behold your glory face to face;
through Jesus Christ your Son our Lord,
who is alive and reigns with you,
in the unity of the Holy Spirit,
one God, now and for ever.

Post Communion

Lord God,
the bright splendour whom the nations seek:
may we who with the wise men
    have been drawn by your light
discern the glory of your presence in your Son,
the Word made flesh, Jesus Christ our Lord.

The Baptism of Christ

The First Sunday of Epiphany

Gold or White

Collect

Eternal Father,
who at the baptism of Jesus
revealed him to be your Son,
anointing him with the Holy Spirit:
grant to us, who are born again by water and the Spirit,
that we may be faithful to our calling
    as your adopted children;
through Jesus Christ your Son our Lord,
who is alive and reigns with you,
in the unity of the Holy Spirit,
one God, now and for ever.

Post Communion

Lord of all time and eternity,
you opened the heavens
    and revealed yourself as Father
in the baptism of Jesus your beloved Son:
by the power of your Spirit
complete the heavenly work of our rebirth
through the waters of the new creation;
through Jesus Christ our Lord.

The Second Sunday of Epiphany

Collect

Almighty God,
in Christ you make all things new:
transform the poverty of our nature
    by the riches of your grace,
and in the renewal of our lives
make known your heavenly glory;
through Jesus Christ your Son our Lord,
who is alive and reigns with you,
in the unity of the Holy Spirit,
one God, now and for ever.

Post Communion

God of glory,
you nourish us with your Word
who is the bread of life:
fill us with your Holy Spirit
that through us the light of your glory
may shine in all the world.
We ask this in the name of Jesus Christ our Lord.

The Third Sunday of Epiphany

Collect

Almighty God,
whose Son revealed in signs and miracles
the wonder of your saving presence:
renew your people with your heavenly grace,
and in all our weakness
sustain us by your mighty power;
through Jesus Christ your Son our Lord,
who is alive and reigns with you,
in the unity of the Holy Spirit,
one God, now and for ever.

Post Communion

Almighty Father,
whose Son our Saviour Jesus Christ
    is the light of the world:
may your people,
illumined by your word and sacraments,
shine with the radiance of his glory,
that he may be known, worshipped, and obeyed
    to the ends of the earth;
for he is alive and reigns, now and for ever.

The Fourth Sunday of Epiphany

Collect

God our creator,
who in the beginning
commanded the light to shine out of darkness:
we pray that the light of the glorious gospel of Christ
may dispel the darkness of ignorance and unbelief,
shine into the hearts of all your people,
and reveal the knowledge of your glory
   in the face of Jesus Christ your Son our Lord,
who is alive and reigns with you,
in the unity of the Holy Spirit,
one God, now and for ever.

Post Communion

Generous Lord,
in word and eucharist we have proclaimed
   the mystery of your love:
help us so to live out our days
that we may be signs of your wonders in the world;
through Jesus Christ our Saviour.

The Presentation of Christ in the Temple

Candlemas

2 February   *Gold or White*

Collect[†]

Almighty and ever-living God,
clothed in majesty,
whose beloved Son
   was this day presented in the Temple,
in substance of our flesh:
grant that we may be presented to you
with pure and clean hearts,
by your Son Jesus Christ our Lord,
who is alive and reigns with you,
in the unity of the Holy Spirit,
one God, now and for ever.

Post Communion

Lord, you fulfilled the hope of Simeon and Anna,
who lived to welcome the Messiah:
may we, who have received these gifts beyond words,
prepare to meet Christ Jesus when he comes
   to bring us to eternal life;
for he is alive and reigns, now and for ever.

The Fifth Sunday Before Lent

Green

This provision is always used from the day after The Presentation of Christ in the Temple until the first of the Sundays before Lent.

Collect

Almighty God,
by whose grace alone we are accepted
     and called to your service:
strengthen us by your Holy Spirit
and make us worthy of our calling;
through Jesus Christ your Son our Lord,
who is alive and reigns with you,
in the unity of the Holy Spirit,
one God, now and for ever.

Post Communion

God of truth,
we have seen with our eyes
     and touched with our hands the bread of life:
strengthen our faith
that we may grow in love for you and for each other;
through Jesus Christ our Lord.

The Fourth Sunday Before Lent

Green

Collect†

O God,
you know us to be set
in the midst of so many and great dangers,
that by reason of the frailty of our nature
we cannot always stand upright:
grant to us such strength and protection
as may support us in all dangers
and carry us through all temptations;
through Jesus Christ your Son our Lord,
who is alive and reigns with you,
in the unity of the Holy Spirit,
one God, now and for ever.

Post Communion

Go before us, Lord, in all we do
with your most gracious favour,
and guide us with your continual help,
that in all our works
begun, continued and ended in you,
we may glorify your holy name,
and finally by your mercy receive everlasting life;
through Jesus Christ our Lord.

The Third Sunday Before Lent

Collect†

Almighty God,
who alone can bring order
to the unruly wills and passions of sinful humanity:
give your people grace
so to love what you command
and to desire what you promise,
that, among the many changes of this world,
our hearts may surely there be fixed
where true joys are to be found;
through Jesus Christ your Son our Lord,
who is alive and reigns with you,
in the unity of the Holy Spirit,
one God, now and for ever.

Post Communion

Merciful Father,
who gave Jesus Christ to be for us the bread of life,
that those who come to him should never hunger:
draw us to the Lord in faith and love,
that we may eat and drink with him
at his table in the kingdom,
where he is alive and reigns, now and for ever.

The Second Sunday Before Lent

Collect

Almighty God,
you have created the heavens and the earth
and made us in your own image:
teach us to discern your hand in all your works
and your likeness in all your children;
through Jesus Christ your Son our Lord,
who with you and the Holy Spirit
    reigns supreme over all things,
now and for ever.

Post Communion

God our creator,
by your gift
the tree of life was set at the heart of the earthly paradise,
and the bread of life at the heart of your Church:
may we who have been nourished at your table on earth
be transformed by the glory of the Saviour's cross
and enjoy the delights of eternity;
through Jesus Christ our Lord.

The Sunday Next Before Lent

Collect

Almighty Father,
whose Son was revealed in majesty
before he suffered death upon the cross:
give us grace to perceive his glory,
that we may be strengthened to suffer with him
and be changed into his likeness, from glory to glory;
who is alive and reigns with you,
in the unity of the Holy Spirit,
one God, now and for ever.

Post Communion

Holy God,
we see your glory in the face of Jesus Christ:
may we who are partakers at his table
reflect his life in word and deed,
that all the world may know
    his power to change and save.
This we ask through Jesus Christ our Lord.

Ash Wednesday

Collect†

Almighty and everlasting God,
you hate nothing that you have made
and forgive the sins of all those who are penitent:
create and make in us new and contrite hearts
that we, worthily lamenting our sins
and acknowledging our wretchedness,
may receive from you, the God of all mercy,
perfect remission and forgiveness;
through Jesus Christ your Son our Lord,
who is alive and reigns with you,
in the unity of the Holy Spirit,
one God, now and for ever.

This Collect may be used as the Post Communion on any day from the First Sunday of Lent until the Saturday after the Fourth Sunday of Lent instead of the Post Communion provided.

Post Communion†

Almighty God,
you have given your only Son to be for us
both a sacrifice for sin
and also an example of godly life:
give us grace
that we may always most thankfully receive
these his inestimable gifts,
and also daily endeavour to follow
    the blessed steps of his most holy life;
through Jesus Christ our Lord.

The First Sunday of Lent

Purple or Lent Array

Collect

Almighty God,
whose Son Jesus Christ fasted forty days in the wilderness,
and was tempted as we are, yet without sin:
give us grace to discipline ourselves
    in obedience to your Spirit;
and, as you know our weakness,
so may we know your power to save;
through Jesus Christ your Son our Lord,
who is alive and reigns with you,
in the unity of the Holy Spirit,
one God, now and for ever.

Post Communion

Lord God,
you have renewed us with the living bread from heaven;
by it you nourish our faith,
increase our hope,
and strengthen our love:
teach us always to hunger for him
    who is the true and living bread,
and enable us to live by every word
    that proceeds from out of your mouth;
through Jesus Christ our Lord.

The Second Sunday of Lent

Purple or Lent Array

Collect[†]

Almighty God,
you show to those who are in error the light of your truth,
that they may return to the way of righteousness:
grant to all those who are admitted
    into the fellowship of Christ's religion,
that they may reject those things
    that are contrary to their profession,
and follow all such things as are agreeable to the same;
through our Lord Jesus Christ,
who is alive and reigns with you,
in the unity of the Holy Spirit,
one God, now and for ever.

Post Communion[†]

Almighty God,
you see that we have no power of ourselves to help ourselves:
keep us both outwardly in our bodies,
and inwardly in our souls;
that we may be defended from all adversities
    which may happen to the body,
and from all evil thoughts
    which may assault and hurt the soul;
through Jesus Christ our Lord.

The Third Sunday of Lent

Purple or Lent Array

Collect

Almighty God,
whose most dear Son went not up to joy
  but first he suffered pain,
and entered not into glory before he was crucified:
mercifully grant that we, walking in the way of the cross,
may find it none other than the way of life and peace;
through Jesus Christ your Son our Lord,
who is alive and reigns with you,
in the unity of the Holy Spirit,
one God, now and for ever.

Post Communion†

Merciful Lord,
grant your people grace to withstand the temptations
  of the world, the flesh and the devil,
and with pure hearts and minds to follow you,
  the only God;
through Jesus Christ our Lord.

The Fourth Sunday of Lent

Purple or Lent Array

Collect†

Merciful Lord,
absolve your people from their offences,
that through your bountiful goodness
we may all be delivered from the chains of those sins
which by our frailty we have committed;
grant this, heavenly Father,
for Jesus Christ's sake, our blessed Lord and Saviour,
who is alive and reigns with you,
in the unity of the Holy Spirit,
one God, now and for ever.

Post Communion

Lord God,
whose blessed Son our Saviour
gave his back to the smiters
and did not hide his face from shame:
give us grace to endure the sufferings of this present time
with sure confidence in the glory that shall be revealed;
through Jesus Christ our Lord.

*Mothering Sunday may be celebrated in preference to the provision for the Fourth
Sunday of Lent.*

Mothering Sunday

Purple or Lent Array

Collect

God of compassion,
whose Son Jesus Christ, the child of Mary,
shared the life of a home in Nazareth,
and on the cross drew the whole human family to himself:
strengthen us in our daily living
that in joy and in sorrow
we may know the power of your presence
    to bind together and to heal;
through Jesus Christ your Son our Lord,
who is alive and reigns with you,
in the unity of the Holy Spirit,
one God, now and for ever.

Post Communion

Loving God,
as a mother feeds her children at the breast
you feed us in this sacrament
    with the food and drink of eternal life:
help us who have tasted your goodness
to grow in grace within the household of faith;
through Jesus Christ our Lord.

*Mothering Sunday may be celebrated in preference to the provision for the Fourth
Sunday of Lent.*

The Fifth Sunday of Lent

Passiontide begins

Purple or Lent Array

Collect

Most merciful God,
who by the death and resurrection of your Son Jesus Christ
delivered and saved the world:
grant that by faith in him who suffered on the cross
we may triumph in the power of his victory;
through Jesus Christ your Son our Lord,
who is alive and reigns with you,
in the unity of the Holy Spirit,
one God, now and for ever.

Post Communion

Lord Jesus Christ,
you have taught us
that what we do for the least of our brothers and sisters
we do also for you:
give us the will to be the servant of others
as you were the servant of all,
and gave up your life and died for us,
but are alive and reign, now and for ever.

Palm Sunday

Collect[†]

Almighty and everlasting God,
who in your tender love towards the human race
   sent your Son our Saviour Jesus Christ
to take upon him our flesh
and to suffer death upon the cross:
grant that we may follow the example
   of his patience and humility,
and also be made partakers of his resurrection;
through Jesus Christ your Son our Lord,
who is alive and reigns with you,
in the unity of the Holy Spirit,
one God, now and for ever.

Post Communion

Lord Jesus Christ,
you humbled yourself in taking the form of a servant,
and in obedience died on the cross for our salvation:
give us the mind to follow you
and to proclaim you as Lord and King,
to the glory of God the Father.

Maundy Thursday

Collect

God our Father,
you have invited us to share in the supper
which your Son gave to his Church
to proclaim his death until he comes:
may he nourish us by his presence,
and unite us in his love;
who is alive and reigns with you,
in the unity of the Holy Spirit,
one God, now and for ever.

At Morning and Evening Prayer the Collect of Palm Sunday is used.

Post Communion

Lord Jesus Christ,
we thank you that in this wonderful sacrament
you have given us the memorial of your passion:
grant us so to reverence the sacred mysteries
   of your body and blood
that we may know within ourselves
and show forth in our lives
the fruit of your redemption,
for you are alive and reign, now and for ever.

Good Friday

Hangings removed: Red for the liturgy

Collect†

Almighty Father,
look with mercy on this your family
for which our Lord Jesus Christ
 was content to be betrayed
 and given up into the hands of sinners
 and to suffer death upon the cross;
who is alive and glorified
 with you and the Holy Spirit,
one God, now and for ever.

Easter Eve

Hangings removed

Collect†

Grant, Lord,
that we who are baptised into the death
 of your Son our Saviour Jesus Christ
may continually put to death our evil desires
 and be buried with him;
and that through the grave and gate of death
we may pass to our joyful resurrection;
through his merits, who died and was buried
 and rose again for us,
your Son Jesus Christ our Lord.

Easter Day

Gold or White

Collect

Lord of all life and power,
who through the mighty resurrection of your Son
overcame the old order of sin and death
to make all things new in him:
grant that we, being dead to sin
and alive to you in Jesus Christ,
may reign with him in glory;
to whom with you and the Holy Spirit
be praise and honour, glory and might,
now and in all eternity.

Post Communion

God of Life,
who for our redemption gave your only-begotten Son
    to the death of the cross,
and by his glorious resurrection
have delivered us from the power of our enemy:
grant us so to die daily to sin,
that we may evermore live with him
    in the joy of his risen life;
through Jesus Christ our Lord.

The Second Sunday of Easter

White

Collect[†]

Almighty Father,
you have given your only Son to die for our sins
and to rise again for our justification:
grant us so to put away the leaven of malice and wickedness
that we may always serve you
in pureness of living and truth;
through the merits of your Son Jesus Christ our Lord,
who is alive and reigns with you,
in the unity of the Holy Spirit,
one God, now and for ever.

Post Communion

Lord God our Father,
through our Saviour Jesus Christ
you have assured your children of eternal life
and in baptism have made us one with him:
deliver us from the death of sin
and raise us to new life in your love,
in the fellowship of the Holy Spirit,
by the grace of our Lord Jesus Christ.

The Third Sunday of Easter

Collect

Almighty Father,
who in your great mercy gladdened the disciples
    with the sight of the risen Lord:
give us such knowledge of his presence with us,
that we may be strengthened and sustained
    by his risen life
and serve you continually in righteousness and truth;
through Jesus Christ your Son our Lord,
who is alive and reigns with you,
in the unity of the Holy Spirit,
one God, now and for ever.

Post Communion

Living God,
your Son made himself known to his disciples
in the breaking of bread:
open the eyes of our faith,
that we may see him in all his redeeming work;
who is alive and reigns, now and for ever.

The Fourth Sunday of Easter

Collect

Almighty God,
whose Son Jesus Christ is the resurrection and the life:
raise us, who trust in him,
from the death of sin to the life of righteousness,
that we may seek those things which are above,
where he reigns with you
in the unity of the Holy Spirit,
one God, now and for ever.

Post Communion

Merciful Father,
you gave your Son Jesus Christ to be the good shepherd,
and in his love for us to lay down his life and rise again:
keep us always under his protection,
and give us grace to follow in his steps;
through Jesus Christ our Lord.

The Fifth Sunday of Easter

Collect[†]
Almighty God,
who through your only-begotten Son Jesus Christ
have overcome death and opened to us
   the gate of everlasting life:
grant that, as by your grace going before us
   you put into our minds good desires,
so by your continual help
we may bring them to good effect;
through Jesus Christ our risen Lord,
who is alive and reigns with you,
in the unity of the Holy Spirit,
one God, now and for ever.

Post Communion
Eternal God,
whose Son Jesus Christ is the way, the truth, and the life:
grant us to walk in his way,
to rejoice in his truth,
and to share his risen life;
who is alive and reigns, now and for ever.

The Sixth Sunday of Easter

Collect
God our redeemer,
you have delivered us from the power of darkness
and brought us into the kingdom of your Son:
grant, that as by his death he has recalled us to life,
so by his continual presence in us he may raise us
   to eternal joy;
through Jesus Christ your Son our Lord,
who is alive and reigns with you,
in the unity of the Holy Spirit,
one God, now and for ever.

Post Communion
God our Father,
whose Son Jesus Christ gives the water of eternal life:
may we thirst for you,
the spring of life and source of goodness,
through him who is alive and reigns, now and for ever.

Ascension Day

Gold or White

Collect[†]

Grant, we pray, almighty God,
that as we believe your only-begotten Son
    our Lord Jesus Christ
to have ascended into the heavens,
so we in heart and mind may also ascend
and with him continually dwell;
who is alive and reigns with you,
in the unity of the Holy Spirit,
one God, now and for ever.

Post Communion

God our Father,
you have raised our humanity in Christ
and have fed us with the bread of heaven:
mercifully grant that, nourished with such spiritual blessings,
we may set our hearts in the heavenly places;
through Jesus Christ our Lord.

The Seventh Sunday of Easter

Sunday after Ascension Day

White

Collect[†]

O God the king of glory,
you have exalted your only Son Jesus Christ
with great triumph to your kingdom in heaven:
we beseech you, leave us not comfortless,
but send your Holy Spirit to strengthen us
and exalt us to the place
    where our Saviour Christ is gone before,
who is alive and reigns with you,
in the unity of the Holy Spirit,
one God, now and for ever.

Post Communion

Eternal God, giver of love and power,
your Son Jesus Christ has sent us into all the world
to preach the gospel of his kingdom:
confirm us in this mission,
and help us to live the good news we proclaim;
through Jesus Christ our Lord.

Day of Pentecost
Whit Sunday

Collect[†]

God, who as at this time
taught the hearts of your faithful people
by sending to them the light of your Holy Spirit:
grant us by the same Spirit
to have a right judgement in all things
and evermore to rejoice in his holy comfort;
through the merits of Christ Jesus our Saviour,
who is alive and reigns with you,
in the unity of the Holy Spirit,
one God, now and for ever.

Post Communion

Faithful God,
who fulfilled the promises of Easter
by sending us your Holy Spirit
and opening to every race and nation
the way of life eternal:
open our lips by your Spirit,
that every tongue may tell of your glory;
through Jesus Christ our Lord.

This Collect and Post Communion are not used on the weekdays after Pentecost.

The Weekdays After the Day of Pentecost

Collect[†]

O Lord, from whom all good things come:
grant to us your humble servants,
that by your holy inspiration
we may think those things that are good,
and by your merciful guiding may perform the same;
through our Lord Jesus Christ,
who is alive and reigns with you,
in the unity of the Holy Spirit,
one God, now and for ever.

Post Communion

Gracious God, lover of all,
in this sacrament
we are one family in Christ your Son,
one in the sharing of his body and blood
and one in the communion of his Spirit:
help us to grow in love for one another
and come to the full maturity of the Body of Christ.
We make our prayer through your Son our Saviour.

Trinity Sunday

Collect[†]

Almighty and everlasting God,
you have given us your servants grace,
by the confession of a true faith,
to acknowledge the glory of the eternal Trinity
and in the power of the divine majesty to worship the Unity:
keep us steadfast in this faith,
that we may evermore be defended from all adversities;
through Jesus Christ your Son our Lord,
who is alive and reigns with you,
in the unity of the Holy Spirit,
one God, now and for ever.

Post Communion

Almighty and eternal God,
you have revealed yourself as Father, Son and Holy Spirit,
and live and reign in the perfect unity of love:
hold us firm in this faith,
that we may know you in all your ways
and evermore rejoice in your eternal glory,
who are three Persons yet one God,
now and for ever.

Day of Thanksgiving for the Institution of Holy Communion

Thursday after Trinity Sunday (Corpus Christi)

White

Collect

Lord Jesus Christ,
we thank you that in this wonderful sacrament
you have given us the memorial of your passion:
grant us so to reverence the sacred mysteries
    of your body and blood
that we may know within ourselves
and show forth in our lives
the fruits of your redemption;
for you are alive and reign with the Father
in the unity of the Holy Spirit,
one God, now and for ever.

Post Communion

All praise to you, our God and Father,
for you have fed us with the bread of heaven
and quenched our thirst from the true vine:
hear our prayer that, being grafted into Christ,
we may grow together in unity
and feast with him in his kingdom;
through Jesus Christ our Lord.

The First Sunday After Trinity

Green

Collect†

O God,
the strength of all those who put their trust in you,
mercifully accept our prayers
and, because through the weakness of our mortal nature
we can do no good thing without you,
grant us the help of your grace,
that in the keeping of your commandments
we may please you both in will and deed;
through Jesus Christ your Son our Lord,
who is alive and reigns with you,
in the unity of the Holy Spirit,
one God, now and for ever.

Post Communion

Eternal Father,
we thank you for nourishing us
with these heavenly gifts:
may our communion strengthen us in faith,
build us up in hope,
and make us grow in love;
for the sake of Jesus Christ our Lord.

The Second Sunday After Trinity

Green

Collect[†]

Lord, you have taught us
that all our doings without love are nothing worth:
send your Holy Spirit
and pour into our hearts that most excellent gift of love,
the true bond of peace and of all virtues,
without which whoever lives is counted dead before you.
Grant this for your only Son Jesus Christ's sake,
who is alive and reigns with you,
in the unity of the Holy Spirit,
one God, now and for ever.

Post Communion

Loving Father,
we thank you for feeding us at the supper of your Son:
sustain us with your Spirit,
that we may serve you here on earth
until our joy is complete in heaven,
and we share in the eternal banquet
with Jesus Christ our Lord.

The Third Sunday After Trinity

Green

Collect

Almighty God,
you have broken the tyranny of sin
and have sent the Spirit of your Son into our hearts
    whereby we call you Father:
give us grace to dedicate our freedom to your service,
that we and all creation may be brought
    to the glorious liberty of the children of God;
through Jesus Christ your Son our Lord,
who is alive and reigns with you,
in the unity of the Holy Spirit,
one God, now and for ever.

Post Communion

O God, whose beauty is beyond our imagining
and whose power we cannot comprehend:
show us your glory as far as we can grasp it,
and shield us from knowing more than we can bear
until we may look upon you without fear;
through Jesus Christ our Saviour.

The Fourth Sunday After Trinity

Collect[†]

O God, the protector of all who trust in you,
without whom nothing is strong, nothing is holy:
increase and multiply upon us your mercy;
that with you as our ruler and guide
we may so pass through things temporal
that we lose not our hold on things eternal;
grant this, heavenly Father,
for our Lord Jesus Christ's sake,
who is alive and reigns with you,
in the unity of the Holy Spirit,
one God, now and for ever.

Post Communion

Eternal God,
comfort of the afflicted and healer of the broken,
you have fed us at the table of life and hope:
teach us the ways of gentleness and peace,
that all the world may acknowledge
the kingdom of your Son Jesus Christ our Lord.

The Fifth Sunday After Trinity

Collect[†]

Almighty and everlasting God,
by whose Spirit the whole body of the Church
    is governed and sanctified:
hear our prayer which we offer for all your faithful people,
that in their vocation and ministry
they may serve you in holiness and truth
to the glory of your name;
through our Lord and Saviour Jesus Christ,
who is alive and reigns with you,
in the unity of the Holy Spirit,
one God, now and for ever.

Post Communion[†]

Grant, O Lord, we beseech you,
that the course of this world may be so peaceably ordered
    by your governance,
that your Church may joyfully serve you
    in all godly quietness;
through Jesus Christ our Lord.

The Sixth Sunday After Trinity

Collect[†]

Merciful God,
you have prepared for those who love you
such good things as pass our understanding:
pour into our hearts such love toward you
that we, loving you in all things and above all things,
may obtain your promises,
which exceed all that we can desire;
through Jesus Christ your Son our Lord,
who is alive and reigns with you,
in the unity of the Holy Spirit,
one God, now and for ever.

Post Communion

God of our pilgrimage,
you have led us to the living water:
refresh and sustain us
as we go forward on our journey,
in the name of Jesus Christ our Lord.

The Seventh Sunday After Trinity

Collect[†]

Lord of all power and might,
the author and giver of all good things:
graft in our hearts the love of your name,
increase in us true religion,
nourish us with all goodness,
and of your great mercy keep us in the same;
through Jesus Christ your Son our Lord,
who is alive and reigns with you,
in the unity of the Holy Spirit,
one God, now and for ever.

Post Communion

Lord God, whose Son is the true vine and the source of life,
ever giving himself that the world may live:
may we so receive within ourselves
    the power of his death and passion
that, in his saving cup,
    we may share his glory and be made perfect in his love;
for he is alive and reigns, now and for ever.

The Eighth Sunday After Trinity

Green

Collect[†]

Almighty Lord and everlasting God,
we beseech you to direct, sanctify and govern
    both our hearts and bodies
in the ways of your laws
    and the works of your commandments;
that through your most mighty protection, both here and ever,
we may be preserved in body and soul;
through our Lord and Saviour Jesus Christ,
who is alive and reigns with you,
in the unity of the Holy Spirit,
one God, now and for ever.

Post Communion

Strengthen for service, Lord,
the hands that have taken holy things;
may the ears which have heard your word
    be deaf to clamour and dispute;
may the tongues which have sung your praise
    be free from deceit;
may the eyes which have seen the tokens of your love
    shine with the light of hope;
and may the bodies which have been fed with your body
    be refreshed with the fullness of your life;
glory to you for ever.

The Ninth Sunday After Trinity

Green

Collect

Almighty God,
who sent your Holy Spirit
to be the life and light of your Church:
open our hearts to the riches of your grace,
that we may bring forth the fruit of the Spirit
in love and joy and peace;
through Jesus Christ your Son our Lord,
who is alive and reigns with you,
in the unity of the Holy Spirit,
one God, now and for ever.

Post Communion

Holy Father,
who gathered us here around the table of your Son
to share this meal with the whole household of God:
in that new world
    where you reveal the fullness of your peace,
gather people of every race and language
    to share in the eternal banquet
    of Jesus Christ our Lord.

The Tenth Sunday After Trinity

Collect[†]
Let your merciful ears, O Lord,
be open to the prayers of your humble servants;
and that they may obtain their petitions
make them to ask such things as shall please you;
through Jesus Christ your Son our Lord,
who is alive and reigns with you,
in the unity of the Holy Spirit,
one God, now and for ever.

Post Communion
God of our pilgrimage,
you have willed that the gate of mercy
should stand open for those who trust in you:
look upon us with your favour
that we who follow the path of your will
may never wander from the way of life;
through Jesus Christ our Lord.

The Eleventh Sunday After Trinity

Collect[†]
O God, you declare your almighty power
most chiefly in showing mercy and pity:
mercifully grant to us such a measure of your grace,
that we, running the way of your commandments,
may receive your gracious promises,
and be made partakers of your heavenly treasure;
through Jesus Christ your Son our Lord,
who is alive and reigns with you,
in the unity of the Holy Spirit,
one God, now and for ever.

Post Communion
Lord of all mercy,
we your faithful people have celebrated that one true sacrifice
    which takes away our sins and brings pardon and peace:
by our communion
keep us firm on the foundation of the gospel
and preserve us from all sin;
through Jesus Christ our Lord.

The Twelfth Sunday After Trinity

Collect[†]

Almighty and everlasting God,
you are always more ready to hear than we to pray
and to give more than either we desire or deserve:
pour down upon us the abundance of your mercy,
forgiving us those things of which our conscience is afraid
and giving us those good things
   which we are not worthy to ask
but through the merits and mediation
of Jesus Christ your Son our Lord,
who is alive and reigns with you,
in the unity of the Holy Spirit,
one God, now and for ever.

Post Communion

God of all mercy,
in this eucharist you have set aside our sins
and given us your healing:
grant that we who are made whole in Christ
may bring that healing to this broken world,
in the name of Jesus Christ our Lord.

The Thirteenth Sunday After Trinity

Collect

Almighty God,
who called your Church to bear witness
that you were in Christ reconciling the world to yourself:
help us to proclaim the good news of your love,
that all who hear it may be drawn to you;
through him who was lifted up on the cross,
and reigns with you in the unity of the Holy Spirit,
one God, now and for ever.

Post Communion

God our creator,
you feed your children with the true manna,
the living bread from heaven:
let this holy food sustain us through our earthly pilgrimage
until we come to that place
   where hunger and thirst are no more;
through Jesus Christ our Lord.

The Fourteenth Sunday After Trinity

Collect

Almighty God,
whose only Son has opened for us
a new and living way into your presence:
give us pure hearts and steadfast wills
to worship you in spirit and in truth;
through Jesus Christ your Son our Lord,
who is alive and reigns with you,
in the unity of the Holy Spirit,
one God, now and for ever.

Post Communion

Lord God, the source of truth and love,
keep us faithful to the apostles' teaching and fellowship,
united in prayer and the breaking of bread,
and one in joy and simplicity of heart,
in Jesus Christ our Lord.

The Fifteenth Sunday After Trinity

Collect

God, who in generous mercy sent the Holy Spirit
    upon your Church in the burning fire of your love:
grant that your people may be fervent
    in the fellowship of the gospel
that, always abiding in you,
they may be found steadfast in faith and active in service;
through Jesus Christ your Son our Lord,
who is alive and reigns with you,
in the unity of the Holy Spirit,
one God, now and for ever.

Post Communion[†]

Keep, O Lord, your Church,
    with your perpetual mercy;
and, because without you our human frailty cannot but fall,
keep us ever by your help from all things hurtful,
and lead us to all things profitable to our salvation;
through Jesus Christ our Lord.

The Sixteenth Sunday After Trinity

Collect[†]

O Lord, we beseech you mercifully to hear the prayers
    of your people who call upon you;
and grant that they may both perceive and know
    what things they ought to do,
and also may have grace and power
    faithfully to fulfil them;
through Jesus Christ your Son our Lord,
who is alive and reigns with you,
in the unity of the Holy Spirit,
one God, now and for ever.

Post Communion

Almighty God,
you have taught us through your Son
that love is the fulfilling of the law:
grant that we may love you with our whole heart
and our neighbours as ourselves;
through Jesus Christ our Lord.

The Seventeenth Sunday After Trinity

Collect

Almighty God,
you have made us for yourself,
and our hearts are restless till they find their rest in you:
pour your love into our hearts and draw us to yourself,
and so bring us at last to your heavenly city
where we shall see you face to face;
through Jesus Christ your Son our Lord,
who is alive and reigns with you,
in the unity of the Holy Spirit,
one God, now and for ever.

Post Communion[†]

Lord, we pray that your grace
    may always precede and follow us,
and make us continually to be given to all good works;
through Jesus Christ our Lord.

The Eighteenth Sunday After Trinity

Green

Collect

Almighty and everlasting God,
increase in us your gift of faith
that, forsaking what lies behind
and reaching out to that which is before,
we may run the way of your commandments
and win the crown of everlasting joy;
through Jesus Christ your Son our Lord,
who is alive and reigns with you,
in the unity of the Holy Spirit,
one God, now and for ever.

Post Communion

We praise and thank you, O Christ, for this sacred feast:
for here we receive you,
here the memory of your passion is renewed,
here our minds are filled with grace,
and here a pledge of future glory is given,
when we shall feast at that table where you reign
with all your saints for ever.

The Nineteenth Sunday After Trinity

Green

Collect[†]

O God, forasmuch as without you
we are not able to please you;
mercifully grant that your Holy Spirit
may in all things direct and rule our hearts;
through Jesus Christ your Son our Lord,
who is alive and reigns with you,
in the unity of the Holy Spirit,
one God, now and for ever.

Post Communion

Holy and blessed God,
you have fed us with the body and blood of your Son
and filled us with your Holy Spirit:
may we honour you,
not only with our lips
but in lives dedicated to the service
    of Jesus Christ our Lord.

The Twentieth Sunday After Trinity

Collect

God, the giver of life,
whose Holy Spirit wells up within your Church:
by the Spirit's gifts equip us to live the gospel of Christ
    and make us eager to do your will,
that we may share with the whole creation
    the joys of eternal life;
through Jesus Christ your Son our Lord,
who is alive and reigns with you,
in the unity of the Holy Spirit,
one God, now and for ever.

Post Communion

God our Father,
whose Son, the light unfailing,
has come from heaven to deliver the world
    from the darkness of ignorance:
let these holy mysteries open the eyes of our understanding
that we may know the way of life,
and walk in it without stumbling;
through Jesus Christ our Lord.

The Twenty-First Sunday After Trinity

Collect[†]

Grant, we beseech you, merciful Lord,
to your faithful people pardon and peace,
that they may be cleansed from all their sins
and serve you with a quiet mind;
through Jesus Christ your Son our Lord,
who is alive and reigns with you,
in the unity of the Holy Spirit,
one God, now and for ever.

Post Communion

Father of light,
in whom is no change or shadow of turning,
you give us every good and perfect gift
and have brought us to birth by your word of truth:
may we be a living sign of that kingdom
where your whole creation will be made perfect
    in Jesus Christ our Lord.

The Last Sunday After Trinity

Collect[†]

Blessed Lord,
who caused all holy scriptures
    to be written for our learning:
help us so to hear them,
to read, mark, learn and inwardly digest them
that, through patience, and the comfort of your holy word,
we may embrace and for ever hold fast
    the hope of everlasting life,
which you have given us in our Saviour Jesus Christ,
who is alive and reigns with you,
in the unity of the Holy Spirit,
one God, now and for ever.

Post Communion

God of all grace,
your Son Jesus Christ fed the hungry
with the bread of his life
and the word of his kingdom:
renew your people with your heavenly grace,
and in all our weakness
sustain us by your true and living bread;
who is alive and reigns, now and for ever.

All Saints' Day

1 November   *Gold or White*

Collect[†]

Almighty God,
you have knit together your elect
in one communion and fellowship
    in the mystical body of your Son Christ our Lord:
grant us grace so to follow your blessed saints
in all virtuous and godly living
that we may come to those inexpressible joys
that you have prepared for those who truly love you;
through Jesus Christ your Son our Lord,
who is alive and reigns with you,
in the unity of the Holy Spirit,
one God, now and for ever.

Post Communion

God, the source of all holiness
    and giver of all good things:
may we who have shared at this table
    as strangers and pilgrims here on earth
be welcomed with all your saints
    to the heavenly feast on the day of your kingdom;
through Jesus Christ our Lord.

The Fourth Sunday Before Advent

Collect

Almighty and eternal God,
you have kindled the flame of love
    in the hearts of the saints:
grant to us the same faith and power of love,
that, as we rejoice in their triumphs,
we may be sustained by their example and fellowship;
through Jesus Christ your Son our Lord,
who is alive and reigns with you,
in the unity of the Holy Spirit,
one God, now and for ever.

Post Communion

Lord of heaven,
in this eucharist you have brought us near
    to an innumerable company of angels
    and to the spirits of the saints made perfect:
as in this food of our earthly pilgrimage
    we have shared their fellowship,
so may we come to share their joy in heaven;
through Jesus Christ our Lord.

The Third Sunday Before Advent

Red or Green

Collect

Almighty Father,
whose will is to restore all things
in your beloved Son, the king of all:
govern the hearts and minds of those in authority,
and bring the families of the nations,
divided and torn apart by the ravages of sin,
to be subject to his just and gentle rule;
who is alive and reigns with you,
in the unity of the Holy Spirit,
one God, now and for ever.

Post Communion

God of peace,
whose Son Jesus Christ proclaimed the kingdom
and restored the broken to wholeness of life:
look with compassion on the anguish of the world,
and by your healing power
make whole both people and nations;
through our Lord and Saviour Jesus Christ.

The Second Sunday Before Advent

Red or Green

Collect[†]

Heavenly Father,
whose blessed Son was revealed
 to destroy the works of the devil
and to make us the children of God and heirs of eternal life:
grant that we, having this hope,
may purify ourselves even as he is pure;
that when he shall appear in power and great glory
we may be made like him
 in his eternal and glorious kingdom;
where he is alive and reigns with you,
in the unity of the Holy Spirit,
one God, now and for ever.

Post Communion

Gracious Lord,
in this holy sacrament
you give substance to our hope:
bring us at the last
to that fullness of life for which we long;
through Jesus Christ our Saviour.

Christ the King

The Sunday Next Before Advent

Red or White

Collect

Eternal Father,
whose Son Jesus Christ ascended to the throne of heaven
 that he might rule over all things as Lord and King:
keep the Church in the unity of the Spirit
and in the bond of peace,
and bring the whole created order to worship at his feet;
who is alive and reigns with you,
in the unity of the Holy Spirit,
one God, now and for ever.

Post Communion[†]

Stir up, O Lord,
the wills of your faithful people;
that they, plenteously bringing forth the fruit of good works,
may by you be plenteously rewarded;
through Jesus Christ our Lord.

*This Post Communion may be used as the Collect at Morning and Evening Prayer
during this week.*

Dedication Festival

Collect

Almighty God,
to whose glory we celebrate the dedication
    of this house of prayer:
we praise you for the many blessings
you have given to those who worship you here:
and we pray that all who seek you in this place
    may find you,
and, being filled with the Holy Spirit,
may become a living temple acceptable to you;
through Jesus Christ your Son our Lord,
who is alive and reigns with you,
in the unity of the Holy Spirit,
one God, now and for ever.

Post Communion

Father in heaven,
whose Church on earth is a sign of your heavenly peace,
an image of the new and eternal Jerusalem:
grant to us in the days of our pilgrimage
that, fed with the living bread of heaven,
and united in the body of your Son,
we may be the temple of your presence,
the place of your glory on earth,
and a sign of your peace in the world;
through Jesus Christ our Lord.

The Holy Days

The Naming and Circumcision of Jesus

1 January   *White*

Collect

Almighty God,
whose blessed Son was circumcised
in obedience to the law for our sake
and given the Name that is above every name:
give us grace faithfully to bear his Name,
to worship him in the freedom of the Spirit,
and to proclaim him as the Saviour of the world;
who is alive and reigns with you,
in the unity of the Holy Spirit,
one God, now and for ever.

Post Communion

Eternal God,
whose incarnate Son was given the Name of Saviour:
grant that we who have shared
    in this sacrament of our salvation
may live out our years in the power
    of the Name above all other names,
Jesus Christ our Lord.

Basil the Great and Gregory of Nazianzus

Bishops, Teachers of the Faith, 379 and 389

2 January   *White*

Collect

Lord God,
whose servants Basil and Gregory
proclaimed the mystery of your Word made flesh,
to build up your Church in wisdom and strength:
grant that we may rejoice in his presence among us,
and so be brought with them to know
the power of your unending love;
through Jesus Christ your Son our Lord,
who is alive and reigns with you,
in the unity of the Holy Spirit,
one God, now and for ever.

Post Communion

Of Teachers of the Faith (see p225)

Aelred of Hexham

Abbot of Rievaulx, 1167

12 January *White*

Collect
Almighty God,
who endowed Aelred the abbot
with the gift of Christian friendship
and the wisdom to lead others in the way of holiness:
grant to your people that same spirit of mutual affection,
so that, in loving one another,
we may know the love of Christ
and rejoice in the eternal possession
    of your supreme goodness;
through Jesus Christ your Son our Lord,
who is alive and reigns with you,
in the unity of the Holy Spirit,
one God, now and for ever.

Post Communion
Of Members of Religious Communities (see p227)

Hilary

Bishop of Poitiers, Teacher of the Faith, 367

13 January *White*

Collect
Everlasting God,
whose servant Hilary
steadfastly confessed your Son Jesus Christ
    to be both human and divine:
grant us his gentle courtesy
to bring to all the message of redemption
    in the incarnate Christ,
who is alive and reigns with you,
in the unity of the Holy Spirit,
one God, now and for ever.

Post Communion
Of Teachers of the Faith (see p225)

Antony of Egypt

Hermit, Abbot, 356

17 January   *White*

Collect

Most gracious God,
who called your servant Antony to sell all that he had
and to serve you in the solitude of the desert:
by his example may we learn to deny ourselves
and to love you before all things;
through Jesus Christ your Son our Lord,
who is alive and reigns with you,
in the unity of the Holy Spirit,
one God, now and for ever.

Post Communion

Of Members of Religious Communities (see p227)

Wulfstan

Bishop of Worcester, 1095

19 January   *White*

Collect

Lord God,
who raised up Wulfstan to be a bishop among your people
    and a leader of your Church:
help us, after his example,
    to live simply,
    to work diligently
    and to make your kingdom known;
through Jesus Christ your Son our Lord,
who is alive and reigns with you,
in the unity of the Holy Spirit,
one God, now and for ever.

Post Communion

Of Bishops (see p226)

Agnes
Child-Martyr at Rome, 304

21 January *Red*

Collect
Eternal God, shepherd of your sheep,
whose child Agnes was strengthened to bear witness
    in her living and her dying
to the true love of her redeemer:
grant us the power to understand, with all your saints,
what is the breadth and length and height and depth
and to know the love that surpasses knowledge,
even Jesus Christ your Son our Lord,
who is alive and reigns with you,
in the unity of the Holy Spirit,
one God, now and for ever.

Post Communion
Of Martyrs (see p224)

Francis de Sales
Bishop of Geneva, Teacher of the Faith, 1622

24 January *White*

Collect
Holy God,
who called your bishop Francis de Sales
to bring many to Christ through his devout life
and to renew your Church with patience and understanding:
grant that we may, by word and example,
reflect your gentleness and love to all we meet;
through Jesus Christ our Saviour,
who is alive and reigns with you,
in the unity of the Holy Spirit,
one God, now and for ever.

Post Communion
Of Teachers of the Faith (see p225)

The Conversion of Paul

25 January   *White*

Collect[†]

Almighty God,
who caused the light of the gospel
to shine throughout the world
through the preaching of your servant Saint Paul:
grant that we who celebrate his wonderful conversion
may follow him in bearing witness to your truth;
through Jesus Christ your Son our Lord,
who is alive and reigns with you,
in the unity of the Holy Spirit,
one God, now and for ever.

Post Communion

Of Apostles and Evangelists (see p223)

Timothy and Titus
Companions of Paul

26 January   *White*

Collect

Heavenly Father,
who sent your apostle Paul to preach the gospel,
and gave him Timothy and Titus
    to be his companions in faith:
grant that our fellowship in the Holy Spirit
may bear witness to the name of Jesus,
who is alive and reigns with you,
in the unity of the Holy Spirit,
one God, now and for ever.

Post Communion

Of Missionaries (see p227)

Thomas Aquinas

Priest, Philosopher, Teacher of the Faith, 1274

28 January *White*

Collect

Eternal God,
who enriched your Church with the learning and holiness
   of your servant Thomas Aquinas:
give to all who seek you
a humble mind and a pure heart
that they may know your Son Jesus Christ
as the way, the truth and the life;
who is alive and reigns with you,
in the unity of the Holy Spirit,
one God, now and for ever.

Post Communion

Of Teachers of the Faith (see p225)

Charles

King and Martyr, 1649

30 January *Red*

Collect

King of kings and Lord of lords,
whose faithful servant Charles
prayed for those who persecuted him
and died in the living hope of your eternal kingdom:
grant us by your grace so to follow his example
that we may love and bless our enemies,
through the intercession of your Son, our Lord Jesus Christ,
who is alive and reigns with you,
in the unity of the Holy Spirit,
one God, now and for ever.

Post Communion

Of Martyrs (see p224)

Anskar

Archbishop of Hamburg, Missionary in Denmark and Sweden, 865

3 February *White*

Collect

God of grace and might,
who sent your servant Anskar
to spread the gospel to the Nordic peoples:
raise up, we pray, in our generation
   messengers of your good news
   and heralds of your kingdom
that the world may come to know
   the immeasurable riches of our Saviour Jesus Christ,
who is alive and reigns with you,
in the unity of the Holy Spirit,
one God, now and for ever.

Post Communion

Of Missionaries (see p227)

Cyril and Methodius

Missionaries to the Slavs, 869 and 885

14 February *White*

Collect

Lord of all,
who gave to your servants Cyril and Methodius
the gift of tongues to proclaim the gospel to the Slavs:
make your whole Church one as you are one
that all Christians may honour one another,
and east and west acknowledge
   one Lord, one faith, one baptism,
and you, the God and Father of all;
through Jesus Christ your Son our Lord,
who is alive and reigns with you,
in the unity of the Holy Spirit,
one God, now and for ever.

Post Communion

Of Missionaries (see p227)

Janani Luwum

Archbishop of Uganda, Martyr, 1977

17 February   *Red*

Collect

God of truth,
whose servant Janani Luwum walked in the light,
and in his death defied the powers of darkness:
free us from fear of those who kill the body,
that we too may walk as children of light,
through him who overcame darkness
    by the power of the cross,
Jesus Christ your Son our Lord,
who is alive and reigns with you,
in the unity of the Holy Spirit,
one God, now and for ever.

Post Communion

Of Martyrs (see p224)

Polycarp

Bishop of Smyrna, Martyr, c.155

23 February   *Red*

Collect

Almighty God,
who gave to your servant Polycarp
boldness to confess the name of our Saviour Jesus Christ
    before the rulers of this world
and courage to die for his faith:
grant that we also may be ready
to give an answer for the faith that is in us
and to suffer gladly for the sake of our Lord Jesus Christ,
who is alive and reigns with you,
in the unity of the Holy Spirit,
one God, now and for ever.

Post Communion

Of Martyrs (see p224)

George Herbert

Priest, Poet, 1633

27 February   *White*

Collect

King of glory, king of peace,
who called your servant George Herbert
from the pursuit of worldly honours
to be a priest in the temple of his God and king:
grant us also the grace to offer ourselves
with singleness of heart in humble obedience to your service;
through Jesus Christ your Son our Lord,
who is alive and reigns with you,
in the unity of the Holy Spirit,
one God, now and for ever.

Post Communion

Of Pastors (see p226)

David

Bishop of Menevia, Patron of Wales, c.601

1 March   *White*

Collect

Almighty God,
who called your servant David
    to be a faithful and wise steward of your mysteries
    for the people of Wales:
in your mercy, grant that,
    following his purity of life and zeal for the gospel of Christ,
we may with him receive the crown of everlasting life;
through Jesus Christ your Son our Lord,
who is alive and reigns with you,
in the unity of the Holy Spirit,
one God, now and for ever.

Post Communion

Of Bishops (see p226)

Chad

Bishop of Lichfield, Missionary, 672

2 March *White*

Collect

Almighty God,
from the first fruits of the English nation
    who turned to Christ,
you called your servant Chad
to be an evangelist and bishop of his own people:
give us grace so to follow his peaceable nature,
    humble spirit and prayerful life,
that we may truly commend to others
the faith which we ourselves profess;
through Jesus Christ your Son our Lord,
who is alive and reigns with you,
in the unity of the Holy Spirit,
one God, now and for ever.

Post Communion

Of Missionaries (see p227)

Perpetua, Felicity and their Companions

Martyrs at Carthage, 203

7 March *Red*

Collect

Holy God,
who gave great courage to Perpetua, Felicity
    and their companions:
grant that we may be worthy to climb the ladder of sacrifice
and be received into the garden of peace;
through Jesus Christ your Son our Lord,
who is alive and reigns with you,
in the unity of the Holy Spirit,
one God, now and for ever.

Post Communion

Of Martyrs (see p224)

Edward King

Bishop of Lincoln, 1910

8 March *White*

Collect

God of peace,
who gave such grace to your servant Edward King
that whomever he met he drew to Christ:
fill us, we pray, with tender sympathy and joyful faith,
that we also may win others
　　to know the love that passes knowledge;
through him who is the shepherd and guardian of our souls,
Jesus Christ your Son our Lord,
who is alive and reigns with you,
in the unity of the Holy Spirit,
one God, now and for ever.

Post Communion

Of Bishops (see p226)

Patrick

Bishop, Missionary, Patron of Ireland, c.460

17 March *White*

Collect

Almighty God,
who in your providence chose your servant Patrick
to be the apostle of the Irish people:
keep alive in us the fire of the faith he kindled
and strengthen us in our pilgrimage
　　towards the light of everlasting life;
through Jesus Christ your Son our Lord,
who is alive and reigns with you,
in the unity of the Holy Spirit,
one God, now and for ever.

Post Communion

Of Missionaries (see p227)

Joseph of Nazareth

19 March   *White*

Collect

God our Father,
who from the family of your servant David
raised up Joseph the carpenter
to be the guardian of your incarnate Son
and husband of the Blessed Virgin Mary:
give us grace to follow him
in faithful obedience to your commands;
through Jesus Christ your Son our Lord,
who is alive and reigns with you,
in the unity of the Holy Spirit,
one God, now and for ever.

Post Communion

Heavenly Father,
whose Son grew in wisdom and stature
in the home of Joseph the carpenter of Nazareth
and on the wood of the cross perfected the work
    of the world's salvation:
help us, strengthened by this sacrament of his passion,
to count the wisdom of the world as foolishness,
and to walk with him in simplicity and trust;
through Jesus Christ our Lord.

Cuthbert

Bishop of Lindisfarne, Missionary, 687

20 March   *White*

Collect

Almighty God,
who called your servant Cuthbert from following the flock
to follow your Son and to be a shepherd of your people:
in your mercy, grant that we, following his example,
may bring those who are lost home to your fold;
through Jesus Christ your Son our Lord,
who is alive and reigns with you,
in the unity of the Holy Spirit,
one God, now and for ever.

Post Communion

Of Missionaries (see p227)

Thomas Cranmer
Archbishop of Canterbury, Reformation Martyr, 1556

21 March   *Red*

Collect

Father of all mercies,
who through the work of your servant Thomas Cranmer
    renewed the worship of your Church
and through his death
    revealed your strength in human weakness:
by your grace strengthen us to worship you
in spirit and in truth
and so to come to the joys of your everlasting kingdom;
through Jesus Christ our Mediator and Advocate,
who is alive and reigns with you,
in the unity of the Holy Spirit,
one God, now and for ever.

Post Communion

Of Martyrs (see p224)

The Annunciation of Our Lord

25 March   *Gold or White*

Collect[†]

We beseech you, O Lord,
pour your grace into our hearts,
that as we have known the incarnation
    of your Son Jesus Christ
by the message of an angel,
so by his cross and passion
we may be brought to the glory of his resurrection;
through Jesus Christ your Son our Lord,
who is alive and reigns with you,
in the unity of the Holy Spirit,
one God, now and for ever.

Post Communion

God most high,
whose handmaid bore the Word made flesh:
we thank you that in this sacrament of our redemption
you visit us with your Holy Spirit
and overshadow us by your power;
strengthen us to walk with Mary the joyful path of obedience
and so to bring forth the fruits of holiness;
through Jesus Christ our Lord.

William Law

Priest, Spiritual Writer, 1761

10 April   *White*

Collect
Almighty God,
who called your servant William Law
to a devout and holy life:
grant that by your spirit of love
and through faithfulness in prayer
we may find the way to divine knowledge
and so come to see the hidden things of God;
through Jesus Christ your Son our Lord,
who is alive and reigns with you,
in the unity of the Holy Spirit,
one God, now and for ever.

Post Communion
Of Teachers of the Faith (see p225)

Alphege

Archbishop of Canterbury, Martyr, 1012

19 April   *Red*

Collect
Merciful God,
who raised up your servant Alphege
to be a pastor of your people
and gave him grace to suffer for justice and true religion:
grant that we who celebrate his martyrdom
may know the power of the risen Christ in our hearts
and share his peace in lives offered to your service;
through Jesus Christ your Son our Lord,
who is alive and reigns with you,
in the unity of the Holy Spirit,
one God, now and for ever.

Post Communion
Of Martyrs (see p224)

Anselm

Abbot of Le Bec, Archbishop of Canterbury, Teacher of the Faith, 1109

21 April   *White*

Collect

Eternal God,
who gave great gifts to your servant Anselm
as a pastor and teacher:
grant that we, like him, may desire you with our whole heart
and, so desiring, may seek you
and, seeking, may find you;
through Jesus Christ your Son our Lord,
who is alive and reigns with you,
in the unity of the Holy Spirit,
one God, now and for ever.

Post Communion

Of Teachers of the Faith (see p225)

George

Martyr, Patron of England, c.304

23 April   *Red*

Collect

God of hosts,
who so kindled the flame of love
in the heart of your servant George
that he bore witness to the risen Lord
by his life and by his death:
give us the same faith and power of love
that we who rejoice in his triumphs
may come to share with him the fullness of the resurrection;
through Jesus Christ your Son our Lord,
who is alive and reigns with you,
in the unity of the Holy Spirit,
one God, now and for ever.

Post Communion

Of Martyrs (see p224)

Mark

Evangelist

25 April   *Red*

Collect

Almighty God,
who enlightened your holy Church
through the inspired witness
    of your evangelist Saint Mark:
grant that we, being firmly grounded
    in the truth of the gospel,
may be faithful to its teaching both in word and deed;
through Jesus Christ your Son our Lord,
who is alive and reigns with you,
in the unity of the Holy Spirit,
one God, now and for ever.

Post Communion

Of Apostles and Evangelists (see p223)

Catherine of Siena

Teacher of the Faith, 1380

29 April   *White*

Collect

God of compassion,
who gave your servant Catherine of Siena
a wondrous love of the passion of Christ:
grant that your people
    may be united to him in his majesty
and rejoice for ever in the revelation of his glory;
who is alive and reigns with you,
in the unity of the Holy Spirit,
one God, now and for ever.

Post Communion

Of Teachers of the Faith (see p225)

Philip and James

Apostles

1 May   *Red*

Collect[†]

Almighty Father,
whom truly to know is eternal life:
teach us to know your Son Jesus Christ
as the way, the truth, and the life;
that we may follow the steps
    of your holy apostles Philip and James,
and walk steadfastly in the way that leads to your glory;
through Jesus Christ your Son our Lord,
who is alive and reigns with you,
in the unity of the Holy Spirit,
one God, now and for ever.

Post Communion

Of Apostles and Evangelists (see p223)

Athanasius

Bishop of Alexandria, Teacher of the Faith, 373

2 May   *White*

Collect

Ever-living God,
whose servant Athanasius testified
    to the mystery of the Word made flesh for our salvation:
help us, with all your saints,
to contend for the truth
and to grow into the likeness of your Son,
Jesus Christ our Lord,
who is alive and reigns with you,
in the unity of the Holy Spirit,
one God, now and for ever.

Post Communion

Of Teachers of the Faith (see p225)

English Saints and Martyrs of the Reformation Era

4 May *White*

Collect

Merciful God,
who, when your Church on earth was torn apart
    by the ravages of sin,
raised up men and women in this land
who witnessed to their faith with courage and constancy:
give to your Church that peace which is your will,
and grant that those who have been divided on earth
    may be reconciled in heaven,
and share together in the vision of your glory;
through Jesus Christ your Son our Lord,
who is alive and reigns with you,
in the unity of the Holy Spirit,
one God, now and for ever.

Post Communion

God, the source of all holiness
    and giver of all good things:
may we who have shared at this table
    as strangers and pilgrims here on earth
be welcomed with all your saints
    to the heavenly feast on the day of your kingdom;
through Jesus Christ our Lord.

Julian of Norwich

Spiritual Writer, c.1417

8 May *White*

Collect

Most holy God, the ground of our beseeching,
who through your servant Julian
revealed the wonders of your love:
grant that as we are created in your nature
    and restored by your grace,
our wills may be so made one with yours
that we may come to see you face to face
and gaze on you for ever;
through Jesus Christ your Son our Lord,
who is alive and reigns with you,
in the unity of the Holy Spirit,
one God, now and for ever.

Post Communion

Of Members of Religious Communities (see p227)

Matthias

Apostle

14 May   *Red*

Collect[†]

Almighty God,
who in the place of the traitor Judas
chose your faithful servant Matthias
to be of the number of the Twelve:
preserve your Church from false apostles
and, by the ministry of faithful pastors and teachers,
keep us steadfast in your truth;
through Jesus Christ your Son our Lord,
who is alive and reigns with you,
in the unity of the Holy Spirit,
one God, now and for ever.

Post Communion

Of Apostles and Evangelists (see p223)

Dunstan

Archbishop of Canterbury, Restorer of Monastic Life, 988

19 May   *White*

Collect

Almighty God,
who raised up Dunstan to be a true shepherd of the flock,
a restorer of monastic life
and a faithful counsellor to those in authority:
give to all pastors the same gifts of your Holy Spirit
that they may be true servants of Christ
    and of all his people;
through Jesus Christ your Son our Lord,
who is alive and reigns with you,
in the unity of the Holy Spirit,
one God, now and for ever.

Post Communion

Of Bishops (see p226)

Alcuin of York
Deacon, Abbot of Tours, 804

20 May *White*

Collect

God of wisdom, eternal light,
who shone in the heart of your servant Alcuin,
revealing to him your power and pity:
scatter the darkness of our ignorance
that, with all our heart and mind and strength,
we may seek your face
and be brought with all your saints
to your holy presence;
through Jesus Christ your Son our Lord,
who is alive and reigns with you,
in the unity of the Holy Spirit,
one God, now and for ever.

Post Communion

Of Members of Religious Communities (see p227)

John and Charles Wesley
Evangelists, Hymn Writers, 1791 and 1788

24 May *White*

Collect

God of mercy,
who inspired John and Charles Wesley
    with zeal for your gospel:
grant to all people boldness to proclaim your word
and a heart ever to rejoice in singing your praises;
through Jesus Christ your Son our Lord,
who is alive and reigns with you,
in the unity of the Holy Spirit,
one God, now and for ever.

Post Communion

Of Pastors (see p226)

The Venerable Bede

Monk at Jarrow, Scholar, Historian, 735

25 May   *White*

Collect

God our maker,
whose Son Jesus Christ gave to your servant Bede
grace to drink in with joy
    the word that leads us to know you and to love you:
in your goodness
grant that we also may come at length to you,
the source of all wisdom,
and stand before your face;
through Jesus Christ your Son our Lord,
who is alive and reigns with you,
in the unity of the Holy Spirit,
one God, now and for ever.

Post Communion

Of Members of Religious Communities (see p227)

Augustine of Canterbury

First Archbishop of Canterbury, 605

26 May   *White*

Collect

Almighty God,
whose servant Augustine was sent as the apostle
    of the English people:
grant that as he laboured in the Spirit
to preach Christ's gospel in this land,
so all who hear the good news
may strive to make your truth known in all the world;
through Jesus Christ your Son our Lord,
who is alive and reigns with you,
in the unity of the Holy Spirit,
one God, now and for ever.

Post Communion

Of Bishops (see p226)

Josephine Butler

Social Reformer, 1906

30 May   *White*

Collect

God of compassion and love,
by whose grace your servant Josephine Butler
followed in the way of your Son
in caring for those in need:
help us like her to work with strength
for the restoration of all
to the dignity and freedom of those created in your image;
through Jesus Christ our Saviour,
who is alive and reigns with you,
in the unity of the Holy Spirit,
one God, now and for ever.

Post Communion

God our redeemer,
who inspired Josephine Butler to witness to your love
and to work for the coming of your kingdom:
may we, who in this sacrament share the bread of heaven,
be fired by your Spirit to proclaim the gospel in our daily living
and never to rest content until your kingdom come,
on earth as it is in heaven;
through Jesus Christ our Lord.

or another Post Communion of 'Any Saint' (p229)

The Visit of the Blessed Virgin Mary to Elizabeth

31 May   *White*

Collect

Mighty God,
by whose grace Elizabeth rejoiced with Mary
and greeted her as the mother of the Lord:
look with favour on your lowly servants
that, with Mary, we may magnify your holy name
and rejoice to acclaim her Son our Saviour,
who is alive and reigns with you,
in the unity of the Holy Spirit,
one God, now and for ever.

Post Communion

Gracious God,
who gave joy to Elizabeth and Mary
as they recognised the signs of redemption
    at work within them:
help us, who have shared in the joy of this eucharist,
to know the Lord deep within us
and his love shining out in our lives,
that the world may rejoice in your salvation;
through Jesus Christ our Lord.

Justin

Martyr at Rome, c.165

1 June   *Red*

Collect

God our redeemer,
who through the folly of the cross taught your martyr Justin
the surpassing knowledge of Jesus Christ:
remove from us every kind of error
that we, like him, may be firmly grounded in the faith,
and make your name known to all peoples;
through Jesus Christ your Son our Lord,
who is alive and reigns with you,
in the unity of the Holy Spirit,
one God, now and for ever.

Post Communion

Of Martyrs (see p224)

Boniface (Wynfrith) of Crediton

Bishop, Apostle of Germany, Martyr, 754

5 June *Red*

Collect

God our redeemer,
who called your servant Boniface
to preach the gospel among the German people
and to build up your Church in holiness:
grant that we may preserve in our hearts
that faith which he taught with his words
    and sealed with his blood,
and profess it in lives dedicated to your Son
Jesus Christ our Lord,
who is alive and reigns with you,
in the unity of the Holy Spirit,
one God, now and for ever.

Post Communion

Of Martyrs (see p224)

Thomas Ken

Bishop of Bath and Wells, Non-Juror, Hymn Writer, 1711

8 June *White*

Collect

O God, from whom all blessings flow,
by whose providence we are kept
and by whose grace we are directed:
help us, through the example of your servant Thomas Ken,
faithfully to keep your word,
humbly to accept adversity
and steadfastly to worship you;
through Jesus Christ your Son our Lord,
who is alive and reigns with you,
in the unity of the Holy Spirit,
one God, now and for ever.

Post Communion

Of Bishops (see p226)

Columba

Abbot of Iona, Missionary, 597

9 June   *White*

Collect

Almighty God,
who filled the heart of Columba
with the joy of the Holy Spirit
and with deep love for those in his care:
may your pilgrim people follow him,
strong in faith, sustained by hope,
and one in the love that binds us to you;
through Jesus Christ your Son our Lord,
who is alive and reigns with you,
in the unity of the Holy Spirit,
one God, now and for ever.

Post Communion

Of Missionaries (see p227)

Barnabas

Apostle

11 June   *Red*

Collect

Bountiful God, giver of all gifts,
who poured your Spirit upon your servant Barnabas
and gave him grace to encourage others:
help us, by his example,
to be generous in our judgements
and unselfish in our service;
through Jesus Christ your Son our Lord,
who is alive and reigns with you,
in the unity of the Holy Spirit,
one God, now and for ever.

Post Communion

Of Apostles and Evangelists (see p223)

Richard

Bishop of Chichester, 1253

16 June *White*

Collect

Most merciful redeemer,
who gave to your bishop Richard a love of learning,
a zeal for souls and a devotion to the poor:
grant that, encouraged by his example,
we may know you more clearly,
   love you more dearly,
   and follow you more nearly,
day by day,
who with the Father and the Holy Spirit are alive and reign,
one God, now and for ever.

Post Communion

Of Bishops (see p226)

Alban

First Martyr of Britain, c.250

22 June *Red*

Collect

Eternal Father,
when the gospel of Christ first came to our land
you gloriously confirmed the faith of Alban
by making him the first to win a martyr's crown:
grant that, following his example,
in the fellowship of the saints
we may worship you, the living God,
and give true witness to Jesus Christ your Son our Lord,
who is alive and reigns with you,
in the unity of the Holy Spirit,
one God, now and for ever.

Post Communion

Of Martyrs (see p224)

Etheldreda

Abbess of Ely, c.678

23 June *White*

Collect

Eternal God,
who bestowed such grace upon your servant Etheldreda
that she gave herself wholly to the life of prayer
    and to the service of your true religion:
grant that we, like her,
may so live our lives on earth seeking your kingdom
that by your guiding
we may be joined to the glorious fellowship of your saints;
through Jesus Christ your Son our Lord,
who is alive and reigns with you,
in the unity of the Holy Spirit,
one God, now and for ever.

Post Communion

Of Members of Religious Communities (see p227)

The Birth of John the Baptist

24 June *White*

Collect[†]

Almighty God,
by whose providence your servant John the Baptist
was wonderfully born,
and sent to prepare the way of your Son our Saviour
by the preaching of repentance:
lead us to repent according to his preaching
and, after his example,
constantly to speak the truth, boldly to rebuke vice,
and patiently to suffer for the truth's sake;
through Jesus Christ your Son our Lord,
who is alive and reigns with you,
in the unity of the Holy Spirit,
one God, now and for ever.

Post Communion

Merciful Lord,
whose prophet John the Baptist
proclaimed your Son as the Lamb of God
    who takes away the sin of the world:
grant that we who in this sacrament have known
    your forgiveness and your life-giving love
may ever tell of your mercy and your peace;
through Jesus Christ our Lord.

Irenæus

Bishop of Lyons, Teacher of the Faith, c.200

28 June   *White*

Collect

God of peace,
who through the ministry of your servant Irenæus
strengthened the true faith
and brought harmony to your Church:
keep us steadfast in your true religion,
and renew us in faith and love,
that we may always walk in the way that leads to eternal life;
through Jesus Christ your Son our Lord,
who is alive and reigns with you,
in the unity of the Holy Spirit,
one God, now and for ever.

Post Communion

Of Teachers of the Faith (see p225)

Peter and Paul

Apostles

29 June   *Red*

Collect

Almighty God,
whose blessed apostles Peter and Paul
glorified you in their death as in their life:
grant that your Church,
inspired by their teaching and example,
and made one by your Spirit,
may ever stand firm upon the one foundation,
Jesus Christ your Son our Lord,
who is alive and reigns with you,
in the unity of the Holy Spirit,
one God, now and for ever.

or, where Peter is celebrated alone

Almighty God,
who inspired your apostle Saint Peter
to confess Jesus as Christ and Son of the living God:
build up your Church upon this rock,
that in unity and peace it may proclaim one truth
and follow one Lord, your Son our Saviour Christ,
who is alive and reigns with you,
in the unity of the Holy Spirit,
one God, now and for ever.

Post Communion

Of Apostles and Evangelists (see p223)

Thomas

Apostle

3 July   *Red*

Collect

Almighty and eternal God,
who, for the firmer foundation of our faith,
allowed your holy apostle Thomas
    to doubt the resurrection of your Son
till word and sight convinced him:
grant to us, who have not seen, that we also may believe
and so confess Christ as our Lord and our God;
who is alive and reigns with you,
in the unity of the Holy Spirit,
one God, now and for ever.

Post Communion

Of Apostles and Evangelists (see p223)

Benedict of Nursia

Abbot of Monte Cassino, Father of Western Monasticism, c.550

11 July   *White*

Collect

Eternal God,
who made Benedict a wise master
in the school of your service
and a guide to many called into community
    to follow the rule of Christ:
grant that we may put your love before all else
and seek with joy the way of your commandments;
through Jesus Christ your Son our Lord,
who is alive and reigns with you,
in the unity of the Holy Spirit,
one God, now and for ever.

Post Communion

Of Members of Religious Communities (see p227)

John Keble

Priest, Tractarian, Poet, 1866

14 July   *White*

Collect
Father of the eternal Word,
in whose encompassing love
all things in peace and order move:
grant that, as your servant John Keble
    adored you in all creation,
so we may have a humble heart of love
for the mysteries of your Church
and know your love to be new every morning,
in Jesus Christ your Son our Lord,
who is alive and reigns with you,
in the unity of the Holy Spirit,
one God, now and for ever.

Post Communion
Of Pastors (see p226)

Swithun

Bishop of Winchester, c.862

15 July   *White*

Collect
Almighty God,
by whose grace we celebrate again
the feast of your servant Swithun:
grant that, as he governed with gentleness
    the people committed to his care,
so we, rejoicing in our Christian inheritance,
may always seek to build up your Church in unity and love;
through Jesus Christ your Son our Lord,
who is alive and reigns with you,
in the unity of the Holy Spirit,
one God, now and for ever.

Post Communion
Of Bishops (see p226)

Gregory and Macrina

Gregory, Bishop of Nyssa, and his sister Macrina, Deaconess, Teachers of the Faith, c.394 and c.379

19 July   *White*

Collect

Lord of eternity, creator of all things,
in your Son Jesus Christ
    you open for us the way to resurrection
that we may enjoy your bountiful goodness:
may we who celebrate your servants Gregory and Macrina
press onwards in faith to your boundless love
and ever wonder at the miracle of your presence among us;
through Jesus Christ your Son our Lord,
who is alive and reigns with you,
in the unity of the Holy Spirit,
one God, now and for ever.

Post Communion

Of Teachers of the Faith (see p225)

Mary Magdalene

22 July   *White*

Collect

Almighty God,
whose Son restored Mary Magdalene
    to health of mind and body
and called her to be a witness to his resurrection:
forgive our sins and heal us by your grace,
that we may serve you in the power of his risen life;
who is alive and reigns with you,
in the unity of the Holy Spirit,
one God, now and for ever.

Post Communion

God of life and love,
whose risen Son called Mary Magdalene by name
and sent her to tell of his resurrection to his apostles:
in your mercy, help us,
who have been united with him in this eucharist,
to proclaim the good news
    that he is alive and reigns, now and for ever.

James

Apostle

25 July   *Red*

Collect†

Merciful God,
whose holy apostle Saint James,
leaving his father and all that he had,
was obedient to the calling of your Son Jesus Christ
and followed him even to death:
help us, forsaking the false attractions of the world,
to be ready at all times to answer your call without delay;
through Jesus Christ your Son our Lord,
who is alive and reigns with you,
in the unity of the Holy Spirit,
one God, now and for ever.

Post Communion

Of Apostles and Evangelists (see p223)

Anne and Joachim

Parents of the Blessed Virgin Mary

26 July   *White*

Collect

Lord God of Israel,
who bestowed such grace on Anne and Joachim
that their daughter Mary grew up obedient to your word
and made ready to be the mother of your Son:
help us to commit ourselves in all things to your keeping
and grant us the salvation you promised to your people;
through Jesus Christ your Son our Lord,
who is alive and reigns with you,
in the unity of the Holy Spirit,
one God, now and for ever.

Post Communion

Father,
from whom every family in heaven and on earth takes its name,
your servants Anne and Joachim revealed your goodness
    in a life of tranquillity and service:
grant that we who have gathered in faith around this table
may like them know the love of Christ
    that surpasses knowledge
and be filled with all your fullness;
through Jesus Christ our Lord.

or another Post Communion for 'Any Saint' (p229)

Mary, Martha and Lazarus

Companions of our Lord

Collect

God our Father,
whose Son enjoyed the love of his friends,
     Mary, Martha and Lazarus,
in learning, argument and hospitality:
may we so rejoice in your love
that the world may come to know
     the depths of your wisdom, the wonder of your compassion,
     and your power to bring life out of death;
through the merits of Jesus Christ,
our friend and brother,
who is alive and reigns with you,
in the unity of the Holy Spirit,
one God, now and for ever.

Post Communion

Father,
from whom every family in heaven and on earth takes its name,
your servants Mary, Martha and Lazarus revealed your goodness
     in a life of tranquillity and service:
grant that we who have gathered in faith around this table
may like them know the love of Christ
     that surpasses knowledge
and be filled with all your fullness;
through Jesus Christ our Lord.

or another Post Communion for 'Any Saint' (p229)

William Wilberforce
Social Reformer, 1833

30 July   *White*

Collect
God our deliverer,
who sent your Son Jesus Christ
to set your people free from the slavery of sin:
grant that, as your servant William Wilberforce
   toiled against the sin of slavery,
so we may bring compassion to all
and work for the freedom of all the children of God;
through Jesus Christ your Son our Lord,
who is alive and reigns with you,
in the unity of the Holy Spirit,
one God, now and for ever.

Post Communion
God our redeemer,
who inspired William Wilberforce to witness to your love
and to work for the coming of your kingdom:
may we, who in this sacrament share the bread of heaven,
be fired by your Spirit to proclaim the gospel in our daily living
and never to rest content until your kingdom come,
on earth as it is in heaven;
through Jesus Christ our Lord.

or another Post Communion for 'Any Saint' (p229)

Oswald
King of Northumbria, Martyr, 642

5 August   *Red*

Collect
Lord God almighty,
who so kindled the faith of King Oswald with your Spirit
that he set up the sign of the cross in his kingdom
and turned his people to the light of Christ:
grant that we, being fired by the same Spirit,
may always bear our cross before the world
and be found faithful servants of the gospel;
through Jesus Christ your Son our Lord,
who is alive and reigns with you,
in the unity of the Holy Spirit,
one God, now and for ever.

Post Communion
Of Martyrs (see p224)

The Transfiguration of Our Lord

6 August   *Gold or White*

Collect

Father in heaven,
whose Son Jesus Christ was wonderfully transfigured
before chosen witnesses upon the holy mountain,
and spoke of the exodus he would accomplish at Jerusalem:
give us strength so to hear his voice and bear our cross
that in the world to come we may see him as he is;
who is alive and reigns with you,
in the unity of the Holy Spirit,
one God, now and for ever.

Post Communion

Holy God,
we see your glory in the face of Jesus Christ:
may we who are partakers at his table
reflect his life in word and deed,
that all the world may know
    his power to change and save.
This we ask through Jesus Christ our Lord.

Dominic

Priest, Founder of the Order of Preachers, 1221

8 August   *White*

Collect

Almighty God,
whose servant Dominic grew in the knowledge of your truth
and formed an order of preachers
    to proclaim the faith of Christ:
by your grace give to all your people a love for your word
and a longing to share the gospel,
so that the whole world may come to know you
and your Son Jesus Christ our Lord,
who is alive and reigns with you,
in the unity of the Holy Spirit,
one God, now and for ever.

Post Communion

Of Members of Religious Communities (see p227)

Mary Sumner

Founder of the Mothers' Union, 1921

9 August *White*

Collect

Faithful and loving God,
who called Mary Sumner to strive
   for the renewal of family life:
give us the gift of your Holy Spirit,
that through word, prayer and deed
   your family may be strengthened and your people served;
through Jesus Christ your Son our Lord,
who is alive and reigns with you,
in the unity of the Holy Spirit,
one God, now and for ever.

Post Communion

Father,
from whom every family in heaven and on earth takes its name,
your servant Mary Sumner revealed your goodness
   in a life of tranquillity and service:
grant that we who have gathered in faith around this table
may like her know the love of Christ
   that surpasses knowledge
and be filled with all your fullness;
through Jesus Christ our Lord.

or another Post Communion for 'Any Saint' (p229)

Laurence

Deacon at Rome, Martyr, 258

10 August *Red*

Collect

Almighty God,
who made Laurence a loving servant of your people
and a wise steward of the treasures of your Church:
fire us with his example to love as he loved
   and to walk in the way that leads to eternal life;
through Jesus Christ your Son our Lord,
who is alive and reigns with you,
in the unity of the Holy Spirit,
one God, now and for ever.

Post Communion

Of Martyrs (see p224)

Clare of Assisi

Founder of the Minoresses (Poor Clares), 1253

11 August   *White*

Collect

God of peace,
who in the poverty of the blessed Clare
gave us a clear light to shine in the darkness of this world:
give us grace so to follow in her footsteps
that we may, at the last, rejoice with her
   in your eternal glory;
through Jesus Christ your Son our Lord,
who is alive and reigns with you,
in the unity of the Holy Spirit,
one God, now and for ever.

Post Communion

Of Members of Religious Communities (see p227)

Jeremy Taylor

Bishop of Down and Connor, Teacher of the Faith, 1667

13 August   *White*

Collect

Holy and loving God,
you dwell in the human heart
and make us partakers of the divine nature
in Christ our great high priest:
help us who remember your servant Jeremy Taylor
to put our trust in your heavenly promises
and follow a holy life in virtue and true godliness;
through Jesus Christ your Son our Lord,
who is alive and reigns with you,
in the unity of the Holy Spirit,
one God, now and for ever.

Post Communion

Of Teachers of the Faith (see p225)

The Blessed Virgin Mary

15 August *White*

Collect

Almighty God,
who looked upon the lowliness of the Blessed Virgin Mary
and chose her to be the mother of your only Son:
grant that we who are redeemed by his blood
may share with her in the glory of your eternal kingdom;
through Jesus Christ your Son our Lord,
who is alive and reigns with you,
in the unity of the Holy Spirit,
one God, now and for ever.

Post Communion

God most high,
whose handmaid bore the Word made flesh:
we thank you that in this sacrament of our redemption
you visit us with your Holy Spirit
and overshadow us by your power;
strengthen us to walk with Mary the joyful path of obedience
and so to bring forth the fruits of holiness;
through Jesus Christ our Lord.

Bernard

Abbot of Clairvaux, Teacher of the Faith, 1153

20 August *White*

Collect

Merciful redeemer,
who, by the life and preaching of your servant Bernard,
rekindled the radiant light of your Church:
grant us, in our generation,
to be inflamed with the same spirit of discipline and love,
and ever to walk before you as children of light;
through Jesus Christ your Son our Lord,
who is alive and reigns with you,
in the unity of the Holy Spirit,
one God, now and for ever.

Post Communion

Of Teachers of the Faith (see p225)

Bartholomew

Apostle

24 August   *Red*

Collect[†]

Almighty and everlasting God,
who gave to your apostle Bartholomew grace
    truly to believe and to preach your word:
grant that your Church
may love that word which he believed
and may faithfully preach and receive the same;
through Jesus Christ your Son our Lord,
who is alive and reigns with you,
in the unity of the Holy Spirit,
one God, now and for ever.

Post Communion

Of Apostles and Evangelists (see p223)

Monica

Mother of Augustine of Hippo, 387

27 August   *White*

Collect

Faithful God,
who strengthened Monica, the mother of Augustine,
    with wisdom,
and through her patient endurance encouraged him
    to seek after you:
give us the will to persist in prayer
that those who stray from you may be brought to faith
in your Son Jesus Christ our Lord,
who is alive and reigns with you,
in the unity of the Holy Spirit,
one God, now and for ever.

Post Communion

Father,
from whom every family in heaven and on earth takes its name,
your servant Monica revealed your goodness
    in a life of tranquillity and service:
grant that we who have gathered in faith around this table
may like her know the love of Christ
    that surpasses knowledge
and be filled with all your fullness;
through Jesus Christ our Lord.

or another Post Communion for 'Any Saint' (p229)

Augustine of Hippo

Bishop of Hippo, Teacher of the Faith, 430

28 August *White*

Collect

Merciful Lord,
who turned Augustine from his sins
    to be a faithful bishop and teacher:
grant that we may follow him in penitence and discipline
till our restless hearts find their rest in you;
through Jesus Christ your Son our Lord,
who is alive and reigns with you,
in the unity of the Holy Spirit,
one God, now and for ever.

Post Communion

Of Teachers of the Faith (see p225)

The Beheading of John the Baptist

29 August *Red*

Collect

Almighty God,
who called your servant John the Baptist
to be the forerunner of your Son in birth and death:
strengthen us by your grace
that, as he suffered for the truth,
so we may boldly resist corruption and vice
and receive with him the unfading crown of glory;
through Jesus Christ your Son our Lord,
who is alive and reigns with you,
in the unity of the Holy Spirit,
one God, now and for ever.

Post Communion

Merciful Lord,
whose prophet John the Baptist
proclaimed your Son as the Lamb of God
    who takes away the sin of the world:
grant that we who in this sacrament have known
    your forgiveness and your life-giving love
may ever tell of your mercy and your peace;
through Jesus Christ our Lord.

John Bunyan

Spiritual Writer, 1688

30 August   *White*

Collect

God of peace,
who called your servant John Bunyan
to be valiant for truth:
grant that as strangers and pilgrims
we may at the last
   rejoice with all Christian people in your heavenly city;
through Jesus Christ your Son our Lord,
who is alive and reigns with you,
in the unity of the Holy Spirit,
one God, now and for ever.

Post Communion

Of Teachers of the Faith (see p225)

Aidan

Bishop of Lindisfarne, Missionary, 651

31 August   *White*

Collect

Everlasting God,
you sent the gentle bishop Aidan
to proclaim the gospel in this land:
grant us to live as he taught
in simplicity, humility, and love for the poor;
through Jesus Christ your Son our Lord,
who is alive and reigns with you,
in the unity of the Holy Spirit,
one God, now and for ever.

Post Communion

Of Missionaries (see p227)

Gregory the Great
Bishop of Rome, Teacher of the Faith, 604

3 September *White*

Collect

Merciful Father,
who chose your bishop Gregory
to be a servant of the servants of God:
grant that, like him, we may ever long to serve you
by proclaiming your gospel to the nations,
and may ever rejoice to sing your praises;
through Jesus Christ your Son our Lord,
who is alive and reigns with you,
in the unity of the Holy Spirit,
one God, now and for ever.

Post Communion

Of Teachers of the Faith (see p225)

The Birth of the Blessed Virgin Mary

8 September *White*

Collect

Almighty and everlasting God,
who stooped to raise fallen humanity
through the child-bearing of blessed Mary:
grant that we, who have seen your glory
    revealed in our human nature
and your love made perfect in our weakness,
may daily be renewed in your image
and conformed to the pattern of your Son,
Jesus Christ our Lord,
who is alive and reigns with you,
in the unity of the Holy Spirit,
one God, now and for ever.

Post Communion

God most high,
whose handmaid bore the Word made flesh:
we thank you that in this sacrament of our redemption
you visit us with your Holy Spirit
and overshadow us by your power;
strengthen us to walk with Mary the joyful path of obedience
and so to bring forth the fruits of holiness;
through Jesus Christ our Lord.

John Chrysostom

Bishop of Constantinople, Teacher of the Faith, 407

13 September *White*

Collect

God of truth and love,
who gave to your servant John Chrysostom
eloquence to declare your righteousness
    in the great congregation
and courage to bear reproach for the honour of your name:
mercifully grant to those who minister your word
such excellence in preaching,
that all people may share with them
in the glory that shall be revealed;
through Jesus Christ your Son our Lord,
who is alive and reigns with you,
in the unity of the Holy Spirit,
one God, now and for ever.

Post Communion

Of Teachers of the Faith (see p225)

Holy Cross Day

14 September *Red*

Collect

Almighty God,
who in the passion of your blessed Son
made an instrument of painful death
to be for us the means of life and peace:
grant us so to glory in the cross of Christ
that we may gladly suffer for his sake;
who is alive and reigns with you,
in the unity of the Holy Spirit,
one God, now and for ever.

Post Communion

Faithful God,
whose Son bore our sins in his body on the tree
and gave us this sacrament to show forth his death
    until he comes:
give us grace to glory in the cross of our Lord Jesus Christ,
for he is our salvation, our life and our hope,
who reigns as Lord, now and for ever.

Cyprian

Bishop of Carthage, Martyr, 258

15 September   *Red*

Collect

Holy God,
who brought Cyprian to faith in Christ,
made him a bishop in the Church
and crowned his witness with a martyr's death:
grant that, after his example,
we may love the Church and her teachings,
find your forgiveness within her fellowship
and so come to share the heavenly banquet
    you have prepared for us;
through Jesus Christ your Son our Lord,
who is alive and reigns with you,
in the unity of the Holy Spirit,
one God, now and for ever.

Post Communion

Of Martyrs (see p224)

Ninian

Bishop of Galloway, Apostle of the Picts, c.432

16 September   *White*

Collect

Almighty and everlasting God,
who called your servant Ninian to preach the gospel
    to the people of northern Britain:
raise up in this and every land
heralds and evangelists of your kingdom,
that your Church may make known the immeasurable riches
    of your Son our Saviour Jesus Christ,
who is alive and reigns with you,
in the unity of the Holy Spirit,
one God, now and for ever.

Post Communion

Of Missionaries (see p227)

Hildegard

Abbess of Bingen, Visionary, 1179

17 September *White*

Collect

Most glorious and holy God,
whose servant Hildegard, strong in the faith,
was caught up in the vision of your heavenly courts:
by the breath of your Spirit
open our eyes to glimpse your glory
and our lips to sing your praises with all the angels;
through Jesus Christ your Son our Lord,
who is alive and reigns with you,
in the unity of the Holy Spirit,
one God, now and for ever.

Post Communion

Of Members of Religious Communities (see p227)

John Coleridge Patteson

First Bishop of Melanesia, and his Companions, Martyrs, 1871

20 September *Red*

Collect

God of all tribes and peoples and tongues,
who called your servant John Coleridge Patteson
to witness in life and death to the gospel of Christ
amongst the peoples of Melanesia:
grant us to hear your call to service
and to respond trustfully and joyfully
to Jesus Christ our redeemer,
who is alive and reigns with you,
in the unity of the Holy Spirit,
one God, now and for ever.

Post Communion

Of Martyrs (see p224)

Matthew

Apostle and Evangelist

21 September *Red*

Collect†

O Almighty God,
whose blessed Son called Matthew the tax-collector
to be an apostle and evangelist:
give us grace to forsake the selfish pursuit of gain
    and the possessive love of riches
that we may follow in the way of your Son Jesus Christ,
who is alive and reigns with you,
in the unity of the Holy Spirit,
one God, now and for ever.

Post Communion

Of Apostles and Evangelists (see p223)

Lancelot Andrewes

Bishop of Winchester, Spiritual Writer, 1626

25 September *White*

Collect

Lord God,
who gave to Lancelot Andrewes
    many gifts of your Holy Spirit,
making him a man of prayer and a pastor of your people:
perfect in us that which is lacking in your gifts,
    of faith, to increase it,
    of hope, to establish it,
    of love, to kindle it,
that we may live in the light of your grace and glory;
through Jesus Christ your Son our Lord,
who is alive and reigns with you,
in the unity of the Holy Spirit,
one God, now and for ever.

Post Communion

Of Bishops (see p226)

Vincent de Paul

Founder of the Congregation of the Mission (Lazarists), 1660

27 September *White*

Collect

Merciful God,
whose servant Vincent de Paul,
by his ministry of preaching and pastoral care,
brought your love to the sick and the poor:
give to all your people a heart of compassion
that by word and action they may serve you
    in serving others in their need;
through Jesus Christ your Son our Lord,
who is alive and reigns with you,
in the unity of the Holy Spirit,
one God, now and for ever.

Post Communion

Of Members of Religious Communities (see p227)

Michael and All Angels

29 September *White*

Collect†

Everlasting God,
you have ordained and constituted the ministries
    of angels and mortals in a wonderful order:
grant that as your holy angels
    always serve you in heaven,
so, at your command,
they may help and defend us on earth;
through Jesus Christ your Son our Lord,
who is alive and reigns with you,
in the unity of the Holy Spirit,
one God, now and for ever.

Post Communion

Lord of heaven,
in this eucharist you have brought us near
    to an innumerable company of angels
    and to the spirits of the saints made perfect:
as in this food of our earthly pilgrimage
    we have shared their fellowship,
so may we come to share their joy in heaven;
through Jesus Christ our Lord.

Francis of Assisi

Friar, Deacon, Founder of the Friars Minor, 1226

4 October *White*

Collect

O God, you ever delight to reveal yourself
to the child-like and lowly of heart:
grant that, following the example of the blessed Francis,
we may count the wisdom of this world as foolishness
and know only Jesus Christ and him crucified,
who is alive and reigns with you,
in the unity of the Holy Spirit,
one God, now and for ever.

Post Communion

Of Members of Religious Communities (see p227)

William Tyndale

Translator of the Scriptures, Reformation Martyr, 1536

6 October *Red*

Collect

Lord, give to your people grace to hear and keep your word
that, after the example of your servant William Tyndale,
we may not only profess your gospel
but also be ready to suffer and die for it,
to the honour of your name;
through Jesus Christ your Son our Lord,
who is alive and reigns with you,
in the unity of the Holy Spirit,
one God, now and for ever.

Post Communion

Of Martyrs (see p224)

Paulinus

Bishop of York, Missionary, 644

10 October   *White*

Collect

God our saviour,
who sent Paulinus to preach and to baptise,
and so to build up your Church in this land:
grant that, inspired by his example,
we may tell all the world of your truth,
that with him we may receive
   the reward you prepare for all your faithful servants;
through Jesus Christ your Son our Lord,
who is alive and reigns with you,
in the unity of the Holy Spirit,
one God, now and for ever.

Post Communion

Of Missionaries (see p227)

Wilfrid of Ripon

Bishop, Missionary, 709

12 October   *White*

Collect

Almighty God,
who called our forebears to the light of the gospel
   by the preaching of your servant Wilfrid:
help us, who keep his life and labour in remembrance,
to glorify your name by following the example
   of his zeal and perseverance;
through Jesus Christ your Son our Lord,
who is alive and reigns with you,
in the unity of the Holy Spirit,
one God, now and for ever.

Post Communion

Of Missionaries (see p227)

Edward the Confessor
King of England, 1066

13 October   *White*

Collect
Sovereign God,
who set your servant Edward
   upon the throne of an earthly kingdom
and inspired him with zeal for the kingdom of heaven:
grant that we may so confess the faith of Christ
   by word and deed,
that we may, with all your saints, inherit your eternal glory;
through Jesus Christ your Son our Lord,
who is alive and reigns with you,
in the unity of the Holy Spirit,
one God, now and for ever.

Post Communion
God our redeemer,
who inspired Edward to witness to your love
and to work for the coming of your kingdom:
may we, who in this sacrament share the bread of heaven,
be fired by your Spirit to proclaim the gospel in our daily living
and never to rest content until your kingdom come,
on earth as it is in heaven;
through Jesus Christ our Lord.

or another Post Communion for 'Any Saint' (p229)

Teresa of Avila
Teacher of the Faith, 1582

15 October   *White*

Collect
Merciful God,
who by your Spirit raised up your servant Teresa of Avila
to reveal to your Church the way of perfection:
grant that her teaching
may awaken in us a longing for holiness,
until we attain to the perfect union of love
in Jesus Christ your Son our Lord,
who is alive and reigns with you,
in the unity of the Holy Spirit,
one God, now and for ever.

Post Communion
Of Teachers of the Faith (see p225)

Ignatius

Bishop of Antioch, Martyr, c.107

17 October   *Red*

Collect

Feed us, O Lord, with the living bread
and make us drink deep of the cup of salvation
that, following the teaching of your bishop Ignatius
and rejoicing in the faith
   with which he embraced a martyr's death,
we may be nourished for that eternal life
   for which he longed;
through Jesus Christ your Son our Lord,
who is alive and reigns with you,
in the unity of the Holy Spirit,
one God, now and for ever.

Post Communion

Of Martyrs (see p224)

Luke

Evangelist

18 October   *Red*

Collect[†]

Almighty God,
you called Luke the physician,
whose praise is in the gospel,
to be an evangelist and physician of the soul:
by the grace of the Spirit
and through the wholesome medicine of the gospel,
give your Church the same love and power to heal;
through Jesus Christ your Son our Lord,
who is alive and reigns with you,
in the unity of the Holy Spirit,
one God, now and for ever.

Post Communion

Of Apostles and Evangelists (see p223)

Henry Martyn

Translator of the Scriptures, Missionary in India and Persia, 1812

19 October   *White*

Collect
Almighty God,
who by your Holy Spirit gave Henry Martyn
a longing to tell the good news of Christ
and skill to translate the Scriptures:
by the same Spirit give us grace to offer you our gifts,
wherever you may lead, at whatever the cost;
through Jesus Christ your Son our Lord,
who is alive and reigns with you,
in the unity of the Holy Spirit,
one God, now and for ever.

Post Communion
Of Missionaries (see p227)

Alfred the Great

King of the West Saxons, Scholar, 899

26 October   *White*

Collect
God, our maker and redeemer,
we pray you of your great mercy
and by the power of your holy cross
to guide us by your will and to shield us from our foes:
that, after the example of your servant Alfred,
we may inwardly love you above all things;
through Jesus Christ your Son our Lord,
who is alive and reigns with you,
in the unity of the Holy Spirit,
one God, now and for ever.

Post Communion
God our redeemer,
who inspired Alfred to witness to your love
and to work for the coming of your kingdom:
may we, who in this sacrament share the bread of heaven,
be fired by your Spirit to proclaim the gospel in our daily living
and never to rest content until your kingdom come,
on earth as it is in heaven;
through Jesus Christ our Lord.

or another Post Communion for 'Any Saint' (p229)

Simon and Jude

Apostles

28 October   *Red*

Collect[†]

Almighty God,
who built your Church upon the foundation
   of the apostles and prophets,
with Jesus Christ himself as the chief corner-stone:
so join us together in unity of spirit by their doctrine,
that we may be made a holy temple acceptable to you;
through Jesus Christ your Son our Lord,
who is alive and reigns with you,
in the unity of the Holy Spirit,
one God, now and for ever.

Post Communion

Of Apostles and Evangelists (see p223)

James Hannington

Bishop of Eastern Equatorial Africa, Martyr in Uganda, 1885

29 October   *Red*

Collect

Most merciful God,
who strengthened your Church by the steadfast courage
   of your martyr James Hannington:
grant that we also,
thankfully remembering his victory of faith,
may overcome what is evil
and glorify your holy name;
through Jesus Christ your Son our Lord,
who is alive and reigns with you,
in the unity of the Holy Spirit,
one God, now and for ever.

Post Communion

Of Martyrs (see p224)

Commemoration of the Faithful Departed

2 November *Purple*

Collect

Eternal God, our maker and redeemer,
grant us, with all the faithful departed,
the sure benefits of your Son's saving passion
   and glorious resurrection
that, in the last day,
when you gather up all things in Christ,
we may with them enjoy the fullness of your promises;
through Jesus Christ your Son our Lord,
who is alive and reigns with you,
in the unity of the Holy Spirit,
one God, now and for ever.

Post Communion

God of love,
may the death and resurrection of Christ
which we have celebrated in this eucharist
bring us, with all the faithful departed,
into the peace of your eternal home.
We ask this in the name of Jesus Christ,
our rock and our salvation,
to whom be glory for time and for eternity.

Richard Hooker

Priest, Anglican Apologist, Teacher of the Faith, 1600

3 November *White*

Collect

God of peace, the bond of all love,
who in your Son Jesus Christ have made the human race
   your inseparable dwelling place:
after the example of your servant Richard Hooker,
give grace to us your servants ever to rejoice
   in the true inheritance of your adopted children
and to show forth your praises now and ever;
through Jesus Christ your Son our Lord,
who is alive and reigns with you,
in the unity of the Holy Spirit,
one God, now and for ever.

Post Communion

Of Teachers of the Faith (see p225)

Willibrord of York

Bishop, Apostle of Frisia, 739

7 November   *White*

Collect

God, the saviour of all,
you sent your bishop Willibrord from this land
to proclaim the good news to many peoples
and confirm them in their faith:
help us also to witness to your steadfast love
    by word and deed
so that your Church may increase
    and grow strong in holiness;
through Jesus Christ your Son our Lord,
who is alive and reigns with you,
in the unity of the Holy Spirit,
one God, now and for ever.

Post Communion

Of Missionaries (see p227)

The Saints and Martyrs of England

8 November   *White*

Collect

God, whom the glorious company of the redeemed adore,
assembled from all times and places of your dominion:
we praise you for the saints of our own land
and for the many lamps their holiness has lit;
and we pray that we also may be numbered at last
with those who have done your will
    and declared your righteousness;
through Jesus Christ your Son our Lord,
who is alive and reigns with you,
in the unity of the Holy Spirit,
one God, now and for ever.

Post Communion

God, the source of all holiness
    and giver of all good things:
may we who have shared at this table
    as strangers and pilgrims here on earth
be welcomed with all your saints
    to the heavenly feast on the day of your kingdom;
through Jesus Christ our Lord.

Leo the Great
Bishop of Rome, Teacher of the Faith, 461

10 November *White*

Collect

God our Father,
who made your servant Leo strong in the defence of the faith:
fill your Church with the spirit of truth
that, guided by humility and governed by love,
she may prevail against the powers of evil;
through Jesus Christ your Son our Lord,
who is alive and reigns with you,
in the unity of the Holy Spirit,
one God, now and for ever.

Post Communion

Of Teachers of the Faith (see p225)

Martin of Tours
Bishop of Tours, c.397

11 November *White*

Collect

God all powerful,
who called Martin from the armies of this world
to be a faithful soldier of Christ:
give us grace to follow him
in his love and compassion for the needy,
and enable your Church to claim for all people
their inheritance as children of God;
through Jesus Christ your Son our Lord,
who is alive and reigns with you,
in the unity of the Holy Spirit,
one God, now and for ever.

Post Communion

Of Bishops (see p226)

Charles Simeon

Priest, Evangelical Divine, 1836

13 November   *White*

Collect

Eternal God,
who raised up Charles Simeon
   to preach the good news of Jesus Christ
and inspire your people in service and mission:
grant that we with all your Church may worship the Saviour,
turn in sorrow from our sins and walk in the way of holiness;
through Jesus Christ your Son our Lord,
who is alive and reigns with you,
in the unity of the Holy Spirit,
one God, now and for ever.

Post Communion

Of Pastors (see p226)

Margaret of Scotland

Queen of Scotland, Philanthropist, Reformer of the Church, 1093

16 November   *White*

Collect

God, the ruler of all,
who called your servant Margaret to an earthly throne
and gave her zeal for your Church and love for your people
that she might advance your heavenly kingdom:
mercifully grant that we who commemorate her example
may be fruitful in good works
and attain to the glorious crown of your saints;
through Jesus Christ your Son our Lord,
who is alive and reigns with you,
in the unity of the Holy Spirit,
one God, now and for ever.

Post Communion

God our redeemer,
who inspired Margaret to witness to your love
and to work for the coming of your kingdom:
may we, who in this sacrament share the bread of heaven,
be fired by your Spirit to proclaim the gospel in our daily living
and never to rest content until your kingdom come,
on earth as it is in heaven;
through Jesus Christ our Lord.

or another Post Communion for 'Any Saint' (p229)

Hugh
Bishop of Lincoln, 1200

17 November *White*

Collect

O God,
who endowed your servant Hugh
with a wise and cheerful boldness
and taught him to commend to earthly rulers
    the discipline of a holy life:
give us grace like him to be bold in the service of the gospel,
putting our confidence in Christ alone,
who is alive and reigns with you,
in the unity of the Holy Spirit,
one God, now and for ever.

Post Communion

Of Bishops (see p226)

Elizabeth of Hungary
Princess of Thuringia, Philanthropist, 1231

18 November *White*

Collect

Lord God,
who taught Elizabeth of Hungary
    to recognize and reverence Christ in the poor of this world:
by her example
strengthen us to love and serve the afflicted and the needy
and so to honour your Son, the servant king,
who is alive and reigns with you,
in the unity of the Holy Spirit,
one God, now and for ever.

Post Communion

Faithful God,
who called Elizabeth of Hungary to serve you
and gave her joy in walking the path of holiness:
by this eucharist
    in which you renew within us the vision of your glory,
strengthen us all to follow the way of perfection
until we come to see you face to face;
through Jesus Christ our Lord.

or another Post Communion for 'Any Saint' (p229)

Hilda

Abbess of Whitby, 680

19 November   *White*

Collect

Eternal God,
who made the abbess Hilda to shine like a jewel in our land
and through her holiness and leadership
    blessed your Church with new life and unity:
help us, like her, to yearn for the gospel of Christ
and to reconcile those who are divided;
through him who is alive and reigns with you,
in the unity of the Holy Spirit,
one God, now and for ever.

Post Communion

Of Members of Religious Communities (see p227)

Edmund

King of the East Angles, Martyr, 870

20 November   *Red*

Collect

Eternal God,
whose servant Edmund kept faith to the end,
both with you and with his people,
and glorified you by his death:
grant us such steadfastness of faith
that, with the noble army of martyrs,
we may come to enjoy the fullness of the resurrection life;
through Jesus Christ your Son our Lord,
who is alive and reigns with you,
in the unity of the Holy Spirit,
one God, now and for ever.

Post Communion

Of Martyrs (see p224)

Clement

Bishop of Rome, Martyr, c.100

23 November   *Red*

Collect

Creator and Father of eternity,
whose martyr Clement bore witness with his blood
to the love he proclaimed and the gospel that he preached:
give us thankful hearts as we celebrate your faithfulness
    revealed to us in the lives of your saints
and strengthen us in our pilgrimage as we follow your Son,
Jesus Christ our Lord,
who is alive and reigns with you,
in the unity of the Holy Spirit,
one God, now and for ever.

Post Communion

Of Martyrs (see p224)

Andrew

Apostle

30 November   *Red*

Collect[†]

Almighty God,
who gave such grace to your apostle Saint Andrew
that he readily obeyed the call of your Son Jesus Christ
    and brought his brother with him:
call us by your holy word,
and give us grace to follow you without delay
    and to tell the good news of your kingdom;
through Jesus Christ your Son our Lord,
who is alive and reigns with you,
in the unity of the Holy Spirit,
one God, now and for ever.

Post Communion

Of Apostles and Evangelists (see p223)

Nicholas

Bishop of Myra, c.326

6 December *White*

Collect

Almighty Father, lover of souls,
who chose your servant Nicholas
    to be a bishop in the Church,
that he might give freely out of the treasures of your grace:
make us mindful of the needs of others
and, as we have received,
    so teach us also to give;
through Jesus Christ your Son our Lord,
who is alive and reigns with you,
in the unity of the Holy Spirit,
one God, now and for ever.

Post Communion

Of Bishops (see p226)

Ambrose

Bishop of Milan, Teacher of the Faith, 397

7 December *White*

Collect

God of hosts,
who called Ambrose from the governor's throne
to be a bishop in your Church
and an intrepid champion of your faithful people:
mercifully grant that, as he did not fear to rebuke rulers,
so we, with like courage,
    may contend for the faith we have received;
through Jesus Christ your Son our Lord,
who is alive and reigns with you,
in the unity of the Holy Spirit,
one God, now and for ever.

Post Communion

Of Teachers of the Faith (see p225)

The Conception of the Blessed Virgin Mary

8 December   *White*

Collect

Almighty and everlasting God,
who stooped to raise fallen humanity
through the child-bearing of blessed Mary:
grant that we, who have seen your glory
    revealed in our human nature
and your love made perfect in our weakness,
may daily be renewed in your image
and conformed to the pattern of your Son
Jesus Christ our Lord,
who is alive and reigns with you,
in the unity of the Holy Spirit,
one God, now and for ever.

Post Communion

God most high,
whose handmaid bore the Word made flesh:
we thank you that in this sacrament of our redemption
you visit us with your Holy Spirit
and overshadow us by your power;
strengthen us to walk with Mary the joyful path of obedience
and so to bring forth the fruits of holiness;
through Jesus Christ our Lord.

Lucy

Martyr at Syracuse, 304

13 December   *Red*

Collect

God our redeemer,
who gave light to the world that was in darkness
by the healing power of the Saviour's cross:
shed that light on us, we pray,
that with your martyr Lucy
we may, by the purity of our lives,
    reflect the light of Christ
and, by the merits of his passion,
    come to the light of everlasting life;
through Jesus Christ your Son our Lord,
who is alive and reigns with you,
in the unity of the Holy Spirit,
one God, now and for ever.

Post Communion

Of Martyrs (see p224)

John of the Cross

Poet, Teacher of the Faith, 1591

14 December *White*

Collect

O God, the judge of all,
who gave your servant John of the Cross
a warmth of nature, a strength of purpose
    and a mystical faith
that sustained him even in the darkness:
shed your light on all who love you
and grant them union of body and soul
in your Son Jesus Christ our Lord,
who is alive and reigns with you,
in the unity of the Holy Spirit,
one God, now and for ever.

Post Communion

Of Teachers of the Faith (see p225)

Stephen

Deacon, First Martyr

26 December *Red*

Collect

Gracious Father,
who gave the first martyr Stephen
grace to pray for those who took up stones against him:
grant that in all our sufferings for the truth
we may learn to love even our enemies
and to seek forgiveness for those who desire our hurt,
looking up to heaven to him who was crucified for us,
Jesus Christ, our mediator and advocate,
who is alive and reigns with you,
in the unity of the Holy Spirit,
one God, now and for ever.

Post Communion

Merciful Lord,
we thank you for the signs of your mercy
revealed in birth and death:
save us by the coming of your Son,
and give us joy in honouring Stephen,
first martyr of the new Israel;
through Jesus Christ our Lord.

John
Apostle and Evangelist

27 December *White*

Collect[†]

Merciful Lord,
cast your bright beams of light upon the Church:
that, being enlightened by the teaching
   of your blessed apostle and evangelist Saint John,
we may so walk in the light of your truth
that we may at last attain to the light of everlasting life;
through Jesus Christ
your incarnate Son our Lord,
who is alive and reigns with you,
in the unity of the Holy Spirit,
one God, now and for ever.

Post Communion

Grant, O Lord, we pray,
that the Word made flesh
proclaimed by your apostle John
may, by the celebration of these holy mysteries,
ever abide and live within us;
through Jesus Christ our Lord.

The Holy Innocents

28 December *Red*

Collect

Heavenly Father,
whose children suffered at the hands of Herod,
though they had done no wrong:
by the suffering of your Son
and by the innocence of our lives
frustrate all evil designs
and establish your reign of justice and peace;
through Jesus Christ your Son our Lord,
who is alive and reigns with you,
in the unity of the Holy Spirit,
one God, now and for ever.

Post Communion

Lord Jesus Christ,
in your humility you have stooped to share our human life
with the most defenceless of your children:
may we who have received these gifts of your passion
rejoice in celebrating the witness of the holy innocents
   to the purity of your sacrifice
   made once for all upon the cross;
for you are alive and reign, now and for ever.

Thomas Becket

Archbishop of Canterbury, Martyr, 1170

29 December   *Red*

Collect

Lord God,
who gave grace to your servant Thomas Becket
to put aside all earthly fear
    and be faithful even to death:
grant that we, disregarding worldly esteem,
may fight all wrong,
uphold your rule,
and serve you to our life's end;
through Jesus Christ your Son our Lord,
who is alive and reigns with you,
in the unity of the Holy Spirit,
one God, now and for ever.

Post Communion

Of Martyrs (see p224)

The Blessed Virgin Mary

Collect

Almighty and everlasting God,
who stooped to raise fallen humanity
through the child-bearing of blessed Mary;
grant that we, who have seen your glory
    revealed in our human nature
and your love made perfect in our weakness,
may daily be renewed in your image
and conformed to the pattern of your Son
Jesus Christ our Lord,
who is alive and reigns with you,
in the unity of the Holy Spirit,
one God, now and for ever.

Post Communion

God most high,
whose handmaid bore the Word made flesh:
we thank you that in this sacrament of our redemption
you visit us with your Holy Spirit
and overshadow us by your power;
strengthen us to walk with Mary the joyful path of obedience
and so to bring forth the fruits of holiness;
through Jesus Christ our Lord.

Apostles and Evangelists

Collect

Almighty God,
who built your Church upon the foundation
    of the apostles and prophets,
with Jesus Christ himself as the chief corner-stone:
so join us together in unity of spirit by their doctrine,
that we may be made a holy temple acceptable to you;
through Jesus Christ your Son our Lord,
who is alive and reigns with you,
in the unity of the Holy Spirit,
one God, now and for ever.

Post Communion

Almighty God,
who on the day of Pentecost
sent your Holy Spirit to the apostles
with the wind from heaven and in tongues of flame,
filling them with joy and boldness to preach the gospel:
by the power of the same Spirit
strengthen us to witness to your truth
and to draw everyone to the fire of your love;
through Jesus Christ our Lord.

or

Lord God, the source of truth and love,
keep us faithful to the apostles' teaching and fellowship,
united in prayer and the breaking of bread,
and one in joy and simplicity of heart,
in Jesus Christ our Lord.

Martyrs

Collect

Almighty God,
by whose grace and power your holy martyr N
triumphed over suffering and was faithful unto death:
strengthen us with your grace,
that we may endure reproach and persecution
and faithfully bear witness to the name
   of Jesus Christ your Son our Lord,
who is alive and reigns with you,
in the unity of the Holy Spirit,
one God, now and for ever.

Post Communion

Eternal God,
who gave us this holy meal
in which we have celebrated the glory of the cross
and the victory of your martyr N:
by our communion with Christ
in his saving death and resurrection,
give us with all your saints the courage to conquer evil
and so to share the fruit of the tree of life;
through Jesus Christ our Lord.

or

God our redeemer,
whose Church was strengthened by the blood of your martyr N:
so bind us, in life and death, to Christ's sacrifice
that our lives, broken and offered with his,
may carry his death and proclaim his resurrection in the world;
through Jesus Christ our Lord.

Teachers of the Faith

Collect

Almighty God,
who enlightened your Church
   by the teaching of your servant *N*:
enrich it evermore with your heavenly grace
and raise up faithful witnesses
who, by their life and teaching,
may proclaim the truth of your salvation;
through Jesus Christ your Son our Lord,
who is alive and reigns with you,
in the unity of the Holy Spirit,
one God, now and for ever.

Post Communion

God of truth,
whose Wisdom set her table
and invited us to eat the bread and drink the wine
   of the kingdom:
help us to lay aside all foolishness
and to live and walk in the way of insight,
that we may come with *N*
   to the eternal feast of heaven;
through Jesus Christ our Lord.

Bishops and Other Pastors

Collect

Eternal God,
you called *N* to proclaim your glory
    in a life of prayer and pastoral zeal:
keep the leaders of your Church faithful
and bless your people through their ministry,
that the Church may grow into the full stature
    of your Son Jesus Christ our Lord,
who is alive and reigns with you,
in the unity of the Holy Spirit,
one God, now and for ever.

or, for a Bishop

Almighty God,
the light of the faithful and shepherd of souls,
who set your servant *N* to be a bishop in the Church,
to feed your sheep by the word of Christ
and to guide them by good example:
give us grace to keep the faith of the Church
and to follow in the footsteps
    of Jesus Christ your Son our Lord,
who is alive and reigns with you,
in the unity of the Holy Spirit,
one God, now and for ever.

Post Communion

God, shepherd of your people,
whose servant *N* revealed the loving service of Christ
    in his/her ministry as a pastor of your people:
by this eucharist in which we share
awaken within us the love of Christ
and keep us faithful to our Christian calling;
through him who laid down his life for us,
but is alive and reigns with you, now and for ever.

Members of Religious Communities

White

Collect

Almighty God,
by whose grace *N*, kindled with the fire of your love,
became a burning and a shining light in the Church:
inflame us with the same spirit of discipline and love,
that we may ever walk before you as children of light;
through Jesus Christ your Son our Lord,
who is alive and reigns with you,
in the unity of the Holy Spirit,
one God, now and for ever.

Post Communion

Merciful God,
who gave such grace to your servant *N*
that he/she served you with singleness of heart
and loved you above all things:
help us, whose communion with you
    has been renewed in this sacrament,
to forsake all that holds us back from following Christ
and to grow into his likeness from glory to glory;
through Jesus Christ our Lord.

Missionaries

White

Collect

Everlasting God,
whose servant *N* carried the good news of your Son
to the people of ... :
grant that we who commemorate his/her service
may know the hope of the gospel in our hearts
and manifest its light in all our ways;
through Jesus Christ your Son our Lord,
who is alive and reigns with you,
in the unity of the Holy Spirit,
one God, now and for ever.

Post Communion

Holy Father,
who gathered us here around the table of your Son
to share this meal with the whole household of God:
in that new world where you reveal
    the fullness of your peace,
gather people of every race and language
to share with *N* and all your saints
in the eternal banquet of Jesus Christ our Lord.

Any Saint

Collect *(general)*

Almighty Father,
you have built up your Church
through the love and devotion of your saints:
inspire us to follow the example of *N*,
whom we commemorate today,
that we in our generation may rejoice with him/her
in the vision of your glory;
through Jesus Christ your Son our Lord,
who is alive and reigns with you,
in the unity of the Holy Spirit,
one God, now and for ever.

or (for Christian rulers)

Sovereign God,
who called *N* to be a ruler among his/her people
and gave him/her grace to be their servant:
help us, following our Saviour Christ
in the path of humble service,
to see his kingdom set forward on earth
and to enjoy its fullness in heaven;
who is alive and reigns with you,
in the unity of the Holy Spirit,
one God, now and for ever.

or (for those working with the poor and underprivileged)

Merciful God,
you have compassion on all that you have made
and your whole creation is enfolded in your love:
help us to stand firm for your truth,
to struggle against poverty,
and to share your love with our neighbour,
that with your servant *N*
we may be instruments of your peace;
through Jesus Christ your Son our Lord,
who is alive and reigns with you,
in the unity of the Holy Spirit,
one God, now and for ever.

or (for men and women of learning)

God our Father,
who gave wisdom and insight to your servant *N*
to fathom the depths of your love
and to understand your design for the world you have made:
grant us the help of your Holy Spirit
that we also may come to a full knowledge of your purposes
revealed in your Son Jesus Christ, our wisdom and our life;
who is alive and reigns with you,
in the unity of the Holy Spirit,
one God, now and for ever.

or (for those whose holiness was revealed in marriage and family life)

Eternal God,
whose love is revealed in the mystery of the Trinity:
help us, like your servant N,
to find in our human loving a mirror of your divine love
and to see in all your children our brothers and sisters in Christ,
who is alive and reigns with you,
in the unity of the Holy Spirit,
one God, now and for ever.

Post Communion

Faithful God,
who called N to serve you
and gave him/her joy in walking the path of holiness:
by this eucharist
    in which you renew within us the vision of your glory,
strengthen us all to follow the way of perfection
until we come to see you face to face;
through Jesus Christ our Lord.

or

God our redeemer,
who inspired N to witness to your love
and to work for the coming of your kingdom:
may we, who in this sacrament share the bread of heaven,
be fired by your Spirit to proclaim the gospel in our daily living
and never to rest content until your kingdom come,
on earth as it is in heaven;
through Jesus Christ our Lord.

or

Father,
from whom every family in heaven and on earth takes its name,
your servant N revealed your goodness
    in a life of tranquillity and service:
grant that we who have gathered in faith around this table
may like him/her know the love of Christ
    that surpasses knowledge
and be filled with all your fullness;
through Jesus Christ our Lord.

or

God, the source of all holiness
    and giver of all good things:
may we who have shared at this table
    as strangers and pilgrims here on earth
be welcomed with all your saints
    to the heavenly feast on the day of your kingdom;
through Jesus Christ our Lord.

The Guidance of the Holy Spirit

Collect

God, who from of old
taught the hearts of your faithful people
by sending to them the light of your Holy Spirit:
grant us by the same Spirit
to have a right judgement in all things
and evermore to rejoice in his holy comfort;
through the merits of Christ Jesus our Saviour,
who is alive and reigns with you,
in the unity of the Holy Spirit,
one God, now and for ever.

or

Almighty God,
you have given your Holy Spirit to the Church
to lead us into all truth:
bless with the Spirit's grace and presence
    the members of this ... *(synod/PCC/etc.)*;
keep us/them steadfast in faith and united in love,
that we/they may manifest your glory
and prepare the way of your kingdom;
through Jesus Christ your Son our Lord,
who is alive and reigns with you,
in the unity of the Holy Spirit,
one God, now and for ever.

Post Communion

God of power,
whose Holy Spirit renews your people
in the bread and wine we bless and share:
may the boldness of the Spirit transform us,
the gentleness of the Spirit lead us,
and the gifts of the Spirit equip us
    to serve and worship you;
through Jesus Christ our Lord.

Rogation Days

Collect

Almighty God,
whose will it is that the earth and the sea
    should bear fruit in due season:
bless the labours of those who work on land and sea,
grant us a good harvest
and the grace always to rejoice in your fatherly care;
through Jesus Christ your Son our Lord,
who is alive and reigns with you,
in the unity of the Holy Spirit,
one God, now and for ever.

or

Almighty God and Father,
you have so ordered our life
    that we are dependent on one another:
prosper those engaged in commerce and industry
and direct their minds and hands
that they may rightly use your gifts in the service of others;
through Jesus Christ your Son our Lord,
who is alive and reigns with you,
in the unity of the Holy Spirit,
one God, now and for ever.

or

God our Father,
you never cease the work you have begun
and prosper with your blessing all human labour:
make us wise and faithful stewards of your gifts
that we may serve the common good,
maintain the fabric of our world
and seek that justice where all may share
    the good things you pour upon us;
through Jesus Christ your Son our Lord,
who is alive and reigns with you,
in the unity of the Holy Spirit,
one God, now and for ever.

Post Communion

God our creator,
you give seed for us to sow and bread for us to eat:
as you have blessed the fruit of our labour in this eucharist,
so we ask you to give all your children their daily bread,
that the world may praise you for your goodness;
through Jesus Christ our Lord.

Harvest Thanksgiving

Green

Collect

Eternal God,
you crown the year with your goodness
and you give us the fruits of the earth in their season:
grant that we may use them to your glory,
    for the relief of those in need
    and for our own well-being;
through Jesus Christ your Son our Lord,
who is alive and reigns with you,
in the unity of the Holy Spirit,
one God, now and for ever.

Post Communion

Lord of the harvest,
with joy we have offered thanksgiving
    for your love in creation
and have shared in the bread and the wine of the kingdom:
by your grace plant within us a reverence for all that you give us
and make us generous and wise stewards
of the good things we enjoy;
through Jesus Christ our Lord.

Mission and Evangelism

Colour of the Season

Collect

Almighty God,
who called your Church to witness
that you were in Christ reconciling the world to yourself:
help us to proclaim the good news of your love,
that all who hear it may be drawn to you;
through him who was lifted up on the cross,
and reigns with you
in the unity of the Holy Spirit,
one God, now and for ever.

Post Communion

Eternal God, giver of love and power,
your Son Jesus Christ has sent us into all the world
to preach the gospel of his kingdom:
confirm us in this mission,
and help us to live the good news we proclaim;
through Jesus Christ our Lord.

The Unity of the Church

Collect

Heavenly Father,
you have called us in the Body of your Son Jesus Christ
to continue his work of reconciliation
and reveal you to the world:
forgive us the sins which tear us apart;
give us the courage to overcome our fears
and to seek that unity which is your gift and your will;
through Jesus Christ your Son our Lord,
who is alive and reigns with you,
in the unity of the Holy Spirit,
one God, now and for ever.

or

Lord Jesus Christ,
who said to your apostles,
'Peace I leave with you, my peace I give to you':
look not on our sins but on the faith of your Church
and grant it the peace and unity of your kingdom;
where you are alive and reign with the Father
in the unity of the Holy Spirit,
one God, now and for ever.

Post Communion

Eternal God and Father,
whose Son at supper prayed that his disciples might be one,
as he is one with you:
draw us closer to him,
that in common love and obedience to you
we may be united to one another
in the fellowship of the one Spirit,
that the world may believe that he is Lord, to your eternal glory;
through Jesus Christ our Lord.

The Peace of the World

Collect

Almighty God,
from whom all thoughts of truth and peace proceed:
kindle, we pray, in the hearts of all, the true love of peace
and guide with your pure and peaceable wisdom
those who take counsel for the nations of the earth
that in tranquillity your kingdom may go forward,
till the earth is filled with the knowledge of your love;
through Jesus Christ your Son our Lord,
who is alive and reigns with you,
in the unity of the Holy Spirit,
one God, now and for ever.

Post Communion

God our Father,
your Son is our peace
and his cross the sign of reconciliation:
help us, who share the broken bread,
to bring together what is scattered
and to bind up what is wounded,
that Christ may bring in the everlasting kingdom of his peace;
who is alive and reigns, now and for ever.

Social Justice and Responsibility

Collect

Eternal God,
in whose perfect realm
no sword is drawn but the sword of righteousness,
and no strength known but the strength of love:
so guide and inspire the work of those who seek your kingdom
that all your people may find their security
in that love which casts out fear
and in the fellowship revealed to us
in Jesus Christ our Saviour,
who is alive and reigns with you,
in the unity of the Holy Spirit,
one God, now and for ever.

or

Almighty and eternal God,
to whom we must all give account:
guide with your Spirit the ... of this *(city, society, etc.)*,
that we/they may be faithful to the mind of Christ
and seek in all our/their purposes to enrich our common life;
through Jesus Christ your Son our Lord,
who is alive and reigns with you,
in the unity of the Holy Spirit,
one God, now and for ever.

Post Communion

Blessed God,
help us, whom you have fed and satisfied in this eucharist,
to hunger and thirst for what is right;
help us, who here have rejoiced and been glad,
to stand with those who are persecuted and reviled;
help us, who here have glimpsed the life of heaven,
to strive for the cause of right
    and for the coming of the kingdom of Jesus Christ,
who is alive and reigns, now and for ever.

Ministry (including Ember Days)

Red or Colour of the Season

Collect *(for the ministry of all Christian people)*

Almighty and everlasting God,
by whose Spirit the whole body of the Church
    is governed and sanctified:
hear our prayer which we offer for all your faithful people,
that in their vocation and ministry
they may serve you in holiness and truth
to the glory of your name;
through our Lord and Saviour Jesus Christ,
who is alive and reigns with you,
in the unity of the Holy Spirit,
one God, now and for ever.

or (for those to be ordained)

Almighty God, the giver of all good gifts,
by your Holy Spirit you have appointed
    various orders of ministry in the Church:
look with mercy on your servants
    now called to be deacons and priests;
maintain them in truth and renew them in holiness,
that by word and good example they may faithfully serve you
to the glory of your name and the benefit of your Church;
through the merits of our Saviour Jesus Christ,
who is alive and reigns with you,
in the unity of the Holy Spirit,
one God, now and for ever.

or (for vocations)

Almighty God,
you have entrusted to your Church
a share in the ministry of your Son our great high priest:
inspire by your Holy Spirit the hearts of many
to offer themselves for the ministry of your Church,
that strengthened by his power,
they may work for the increase of your kingdom
and set forward the eternal praise of your name;
through Jesus Christ your Son our Lord,
who is alive and reigns with you,
in the unity of the Holy Spirit,
one God, now and for ever.

or (for the inauguration of a new ministry)

God our Father, Lord of all the world,
through your Son you have called us into the fellowship
    of your universal Church:
hear our prayer for your faithful people
that in their vocation and ministry
each may be an instrument of your love,
and give to your servant *N* now to be ... *(installed, inducted, etc.)*
the needful gifts of grace;
through our Lord and Saviour Jesus Christ,
who is alive and reigns with you,
in the unity of the Holy Spirit,
one God, now and for ever.

Post Communion

Heavenly Father,
whose ascended Son gave gifts of leadership and service
    to the Church:
strengthen us who have received this holy food
to be good stewards of your manifold grace,
through him who came not to be served but to serve,
    and give his life as a ransom for many,
Jesus Christ our Lord.

or

Lord of the harvest,
you have fed your people in this sacrament
with the fruits of creation made holy by your Spirit:
by your grace raise up among us faithful labourers
to sow your word and reap the harvest of souls;
through Jesus Christ our Lord.

In Time of Trouble

Colour of the Season

Collect

Sovereign God,
the defence of those who trust in you
and the strength of those who suffer:
look with mercy on our affliction
and deliver us through our mighty Saviour Jesus Christ,
who is alive and reigns with you,
in the unity of the Holy Spirit,
one God, now and for ever.

Post Communion

Almighty God,
whose Son gave us in this meal a pledge of your saving love
and a foretaste of your kingdom of justice and peace:
strengthen your people in their faith
that they may endure the sufferings of this present time
in expectation of the glory to be revealed;
through Jesus Christ our Lord.

For the Sovereign

Colour of the Season

Collect

Almighty God,
the fountain of all goodness,
bless our Sovereign Lady, Queen Elizabeth,
and all who are in authority under her;
that they may order all things
   in wisdom and equity, righteousness and peace,
to the honour and glory of your name
and the good of your Church and people;
through Jesus Christ your Son our Lord,
who is alive and reigns with you,
in the unity of the Holy Spirit,
one God, now and for ever.

Post Communion

O God, the Father of our Lord Jesus Christ,
our only Saviour, the prince of peace:
give us grace seriously to lay to heart
the great dangers we are in by our unhappy divisions;
take away our hatred and prejudice
and whatever else may hinder us from godly union and concord,
that, as there is but one body, one Spirit
   and one hope of our calling,
one Lord, one faith, one baptism,
one God and Father of us all,
so may we henceforth be all of one heart and of one soul,
united in one holy bond of truth and peace, of faith and charity,
and may with one mind and one mouth glorify you;
through Jesus Christ our Lord.

COMMENTARY
AND SOURCES

The Calendar

The Seasons

Principles

The shape of the calendar of the Christian year naturally precedes any detailed consideration of the lectionary. Readings are chosen and arranged, not only to ensure a wide and balanced reading of Scripture, but also to enhance the celebration of the cycle of the Christian year. The Revised Common Lectionary (RCL), which has been adapted for use in the Church of England, is in general accord with four calendar principles.

- The calendar celebrates and proclaims the Christian belief in God the Holy Trinity, Father Son and Spirit, and tells the story of the saving work of Christ in such a way that Christian people today may be helped in their spiritual life and their discipleship.

- The calendar is, as far as possible, in line with the current practice of the Western Church, and especially with the practice of other Anglican provinces.

- The calendar only departs from the calendar of *The Book of Common Prayer* for serious reason, since one calendar in the Church of England for as much of the year as possible is desirable.

- The calendar gives expression to some of the insights on the shape of the Christian year tested in recent years (especially in relation to All Saints' tide, Epiphany and the period from Easter to Pentecost).

The Major Features of the Calendar

Sundays 'of'

In the seasons of Christmas, Epiphany and Easter, Sundays are called Sundays 'of' the season, rather than 'after'. 'After' works against the intention of the calendar and the lectionary to sustain the spirit of the season through a period of several weeks. 'The Second Sunday of Easter' sounds a different note than 'The First Sunday after Easter'. For consistency's sake, Advent and Lent are also given Sundays 'of'. The time after the Feast of Pentecost and Trinity Sunday is a different case. It is a non-seasonal time, and 'after' is appropriate rather than 'of'.

The beginning of the year

The Christian year begins on the First Sunday of Advent, four weeks before Christmas. This abandons the ASB's Sundays before Christmas and returns to the traditional pattern.

Epiphany

The season of Epiphany, as a gradual unfolding of the mystery of the incarnation and of the revelation of the person of Jesus Christ, extends until the fortieth day after Christmas Day, 2 February, the Presentation of Christ in the Temple. February 2 marks the end of Epiphany and a return to ordinary time (see below), whatever the date of Easter.

Passiontide
In Lent, there is a 'change of gear' on the Fifth Sunday in Lent into a period called Passiontide. To have no change until Palm Sunday itself is not always satisfactory and an earlier week to run up to Palm Sunday is helpful and well established. However, bearing in mind that Palm Sunday is the Sunday of the Passion, the title for the previous Sunday is the Fifth Sunday of Lent, as in *The Book of Common Prayer* and *The Alternative Service Book*.

The Great Fifty Days
The fifty-day period from Easter Day to Pentecost is one season, in which the paschal mystery of the death, resurrection and ascension of the Lord and the coming of the Spirit are explored and celebrated. The final nine days, between Ascension Day and Pentecost, are still part of the Easter season but are, in effect, a Pentecost sub-season, introducing Holy Spirit material in preparation for the Feast of Pentecost, the celebration of the outpouring of the Holy Spirit, with which the season ends. Ordinary time resumes on the day after the Feast of Pentecost.

Ordinary time
The periods between the Presentation and Ash Wednesday, and between Pentecost and the First Sunday of Advent, are regarded as ordinary time, with no seasonal emphasis or predetermined themes, except for an emphasis on the reign of Christ in earth and heaven in the weeks after All Saints' Day (see below).

Sundays after Trinity
Sundays during the summer period of ordinary time are designated 'Sundays after *Trinity*'. This is partly in order to avoid an unnecessary clash of titles through a major part of the year and to stay with the BCP calendar. It also reflects a long, until recently unbroken, tradition in these islands, and serves to affirm the Trinity not as a dry dusty doctrine, but as a vital part of Christian life and worship. An agreed ecumenical naming of Sundays is not easily achieved.

Sundays before Advent
In the period from All Saints' Day to Advent Sunday, Sundays are designated 'before Advent', and bring together a cluster of themes that November provides – All Saints', the Departed, Remembrance and the Kingship of Christ. This brings the Christian year to an end with a celebration both of the reality of God's rule and of the final ingathering into his kingdom. The need for a strong Christian awareness of these truths, to counter the secular culture at this time of the year, with Hallowe'en and its ghosts and witches, has never been greater. In the cycle of the seasons such an emphasis at the end of the year leads very naturally into the beginning of the new year, the season of Advent, when the same theme is developed from a slightly different angle. There is a long history of pre-Advent material that begins to anticipate what is to come, not least

in the BCP provision for the Last Sunday after Trinity.

Principal Feasts

The feasts of the Church should be celebrated at a time when the Christian community is able to come together. Where Christians are able to gather on weekdays for festivals such as All Saints' Day or The Presentation, that remains desirable, but the proposals make it possible for certain days to be transferred to a Sunday. For a major mood change of the Christian year to be celebrated by only a small minority of the local congregation is clearly unhelpful.

The Feast of the Presentation celebrates a major gospel event of theological significance. It marks the end of the forty days incarnation cycle and a first turning towards Christ's passion. It is listed as a principal feast.

Ember Days

The Liturgical Commission proposes a shift in the emphasis of Ember Days. While allowing for them on their traditional days, the calendar encourages the diocesan bishop to set Ember Days in the week before he ordains.

The Holy Days

Principles

- The Church is encouraged and enriched by the celebration of its fellowship with saints and heroes through the generations.

- The celebration of the saints must not detract from the cycle of the Christian seasons or the observance of Sunday as the day of the Lord's resurrection, but *some* celebration of saints on Sundays (especially in ordinary time) is to be allowed.

- A simple system of categorization (not of sanctity, but of observance) is helpful. Three categories (other than principal feasts) have been identified and their level of observance indicated: festivals, lesser festivals and commemorations.

- The Church of England does not canonize and does not, by including a name in a calendar, make any claim about the present heavenly state of the person. It is therefore restrained in what it says about them in its liturgical texts.

Dates

As far as possible, the proposals opt for the date on which the Roman Catholic Church in England and Wales also keeps a particular saint. It seems unhelpful for two churches in the same land to celebrate the same saints on different days, and we have noted that proposals in that Church also seek to find a common date with us. We have, however, noted long-established celebrations (for example, in March of St Chad and St Cuthbert) and retained their traditional dates, even though the Church of Rome has moved these festivals to the autumn. The dates from the Roman Calendar are suggested as alternatives.

There has been an effort to reduce the number of saints' days in Advent and Lent and in the early days of Christmas and Easter in order not to detract from the season. But some saints' days remain in that period, especially ones that do not detract from the season but are very much part of it, such as Nicholas and Lucy in Advent, or the martyrs Polycarp or Perpetua in Lent.

Dates for new entries have been chosen for various reasons: dates of birth, of baptism, of ordination or of death, or sometimes the day of a particularly significant moment in a person's life (for instance, John Keble on the day of his Assize Sermon) where the day of birth or death is at an unsuitable time of year or already occupied by another observance.

Festivals

The days designated as 'festivals' are the same as in the ASB, except for seven:

- The First Sunday of Epiphany (or when 6 January is a Sunday, 7 January) is designated the Baptism of Christ.

- St George's Day (23 April) is made a festival to encourage wider celebration of the Feast of England's patron saint.

- The Visit of Mary to Elizabeth (31 May) celebrates an important and attractive event described in the Gospels, and it allows for a festival of Mary away from the summer holiday period.

- Most recent Anglican provision designates 29 June 'St Peter and St Paul'. The possibility of St Peter alone is allowed in collect and lectionary provision.

- The main festival of the Blessed Virgin Mary is 15 August. It was a last-minute move in the process of calendar provision for the ASB that it was placed on 8 September (the traditional observance of her birth), but the rest of our Communion has not followed us in this respect. The title of the day 'The Blessed Virgin Mary' and the liturgical provision for that day avoid any unacceptable doctrinal implications.

- Holy Cross Day (14 September) is designated as a festival. Many observe it as such already, and there is value in a day that celebrates and reflects on the cross of Christ away from the particular mood of Holy Week.

- The Sunday Next Before Advent is designated the Feast of Christ the King. It is a fitting climax to the liturgical cycle.

Lesser Festivals: Criteria of Sanctity

When a Church decides on a list of those whom it wishes to commemorate in its worship, it is in fact making a statement about the way in which it understands its relationship to the universal Church, to the particular Communion of which it is a part, and to the country or culture in which it is set. There are at least four aspects to such a statement:

Communion

A recognition of the universal nature of the body of Christ, and of the living fellowship of that divided body across all frontiers of space, time and denomination.

Inspiration
Those who stir us to renewed fellowship in the faith are commemorated. They may be people around whom significant events have taken place in the story of the Church. They may be people in whose lives the light of Christ has shone, and who renew in us the sense of God's holiness.

Reconciliation
Commemorations may witness to past and continuing rifts and divisions within the community of faith and to the prayer that they may be overcome.

Celebration
Particular Christian communities will wish to remember those who are honoured in their locality as 'heroes' of the faith.

Lesser Festivals: The Fifty-Year Rule
The established Anglican convention of not including among the lesser festivals the names of any who have died in the last fifty years has been followed, except for those who have died a martyr's death. Whereas it takes time and testing to discover whether a person's life has such a quality of heroic sanctity that the Church ought to regard them as models, one who dies as a martyr witnesses by his or her death. The sanctity of the life that went before it, though not irrelevant, is not the issue.

In our own day the Church has had its martyrs and some of these are included without waiting for the fifty-year rule to run its course.

Groups
Sanctity is perhaps best remembered and celebrated in relation to individuals and their stories, rather than in relation to vast geographical areas. Names such as Anskar, Cyril and Methodius, Willibrord, John Coleridge Patteson and Henry Martyn among the lesser festivals reflect this concern in preference to the ASB group commemorations.

One group commemoration other than the long-established Saints and Martyrs of England remains, namely the English Saints and Martyrs of the Reformation Era on 4 May. This is the designation and the date used by the Roman Church in England, and it seems appropriate, across the Reformation divide, to celebrate this on the same day. There are also days for some named individuals with a particular place in our history.

Commemorations
The calendar includes a category of 'commemorations' which does not envisage that these be kept as holy days, but that mention might be made of those named in prayers of intercession and thanksgiving. Although there is a flexibility that allows them to be regarded as lesser festivals, this is to be the exception rather than the norm.

By their inclusion a small step is taken in making their stories known. If these stories inspire the Church today, then the question will arise whether they should be included among the lesser festivals. The Church may come to provide a way for names to be brought into the calendar as lesser festivals or commemorations at times other than when service books are being revised.

The Lectionary

The Seasons

The Revised Common Lectionary

The Revised Common Lectionary (RCL) is used as the principal Sunday service lectionary, alternative to the eucharistic lectionary of *The Book of Common Prayer*. The expectation is that the RCL be used for the principal service, whether eucharistic or not.

Those who wish to understand more fully the principles on which the RCL has been devised and the recent lectionary history that has led to its publication should study *The Revised Common Lectionary: The Consultation on Common Texts* (Canterbury Press, 1992) and in particular the introduction to the RCL in that book.

In outline, the Revised Common Lectionary is a three-year lectionary cycle, with three readings and a psalm for each Sunday. In each year one of the synoptic Gospels predominates, with a semi-continuous approach to reading it, especially in ordinary time. Other books of the Bible are also read semi-continuously at appropriate seasons as well as in ordinary time. The lectionary is seasonal, but not often thematic.

Themes

The Church of England has grown used to a thematic approach to the reading of Scripture through the ASB lectionary and the published material to support it. Over the years two things have emerged: the narrowness of the themes which have worn thin and do not bear much repetition; and the reading of Scripture through predetermined themes rather than with openness. Every service and every sermon will have a theme (or themes), but they emerge from a creative use of Scripture and liturgy by those planning worship, rather than pre-determining them. The RCL approach stays with a biblical book long enough to understand its underlying shape, message and emphasis.

Why the RCL?

The RCL has been adopted for the following reasons:

- its approach to the reading of Scripture
- the range and balance of Scripture over three years
- ecumenical considerations. The RCL is similar to, though not identical with, that of the Roman Church, and has been adopted by Anglican and other Churches in many countries

- the Scottish Episcopal Church and the Church in Wales have adopted it, and many other denominations in this country are doing so

- it has been tested by a number of cathedrals, churches and religious communities, albeit for a short while, and the majority have been satisfied, though challenged, by it.

Areas of Concern

It has been important not to alter the RCL to the extent that it ceases to be a common lectionary and becomes something eccentrically Church of England. There are, however, a number of modifications:

Omission of verses

There is some disquiet that in a desire to prevent a reading being too long or unhelpful, verses are omitted. All but the most obscure omitted verses have been restored in a bracketed form that allows their use by those who wish to do so.

Shorter psalmody

Some alternative shorter psalm provision is made. At the eucharist it is often appropriate to use only six or eight verses.

Calendar requirements

A few alterations to the RCL have been made in the weeks of Epiphany and before Advent to ensure that the lectionary enriches the seasonal emphasis. These changes are minimal except in Year B in Epiphany where, for three Sundays, readings from Revelation replace readings from 1 Corinthians.

Creation

The treatment of creation in the RCL is surprisingly small, with minimal use of Genesis 1 and 2 outside the Easter Vigil. Celebration and reflection upon creation, in ways different from harvest, have led to provision of a set of readings for use on the Second Sunday before Lent (close to the old identification of Septuagesima with creation) different from the RCL. The RCL observes a Transfiguration Sunday on the Sunday Next Before Lent. The lectionary now moves from creation, to transfiguration, and then into the season that prepares to celebrate our redemption.

The Old Testament in the Easter season

The RCL, like the Roman lectionary, has the first reading from Acts in Eastertide, and the second from an epistle. The Old Testament is therefore not read in the Easter season. There will sometimes be a need for OT provision (if, for instance, the lectionary is being used at BCP Morning Prayer) and there will, in any case, be those unhappy to go without the Old Testament at the eucharist. A note allows the use on Sundays of Eastertide of the generous provision of OT readings in the Easter Vigil (including, in Year A, the story of the Flood over three weeks). A table (p60) shows how this may best be done. To go beyond that would undermine a common lectionary in an important season.

Bible Sunday

Use of the RCL does not accord well with the Second Sunday of Advent as Bible Sunday. Even without following the RCL, there is a strong case for moving that observance to the Last Sunday after Trinity or another date of the minister's choice. The Church in Wales has made a similar move.

Lectionaries for a Second and a Third Sunday Service

The RCL provides only one set of Sunday readings, while Church of England churches frequently need two or even three. The RCL is for use at the *Principal Service* of each Sunday (in most communities the Sunday mid-morning service). The *Second Service* (in many communities the Sunday evening service) will sometimes be eucharistic, and so provision has always been made for a Gospel reading in this service. The *Third Service* provision (which not every church will use) will meet two needs: firstly, the need for a Sunday Office lectionary (for example, for Morning Prayer before a celebration of Holy Communion); secondly, the need for a third major liturgy of the day (for example, sung Morning Prayer in those places where there is also a sung eucharist).

The provision of lectionaries for a Second and a Third Service has been devised to supplement the RCL. It proceeds along similar lectionary principles. The main intention is always to complement the RCL. In the seasons, it sets out to reflect the same seasonal emphasis as the RCL, adding to the Scriptures (including psalmody) appropriate to the particular season and using passages to be found in the RCL in years when the RCL omits them. In ordinary time, there is no attempt to relate the psalmody to the readings (and nearly all the psalms not used during the seasons and in the RCL in a particular year are used in course), nor is there any attempt to relate the first reading to the second. The provision follows a three-year cycle, like the RCL, but in the Third Service the readings in ordinary time are the same in all three years.

The psalm provision in ordinary time has, as far as possible, been arranged so that, when a psalm is used in some years in the Second Service provision, in other years it will be used in the Third Service provision. For the Second Service, some longer portions of psalmody have been appointed in recognition of a need for this in some churches, but a shorter alternative is always given.

Alternative Lectionary Provision

The RCL is recommended as the *normative* lectionary provision. However, there is a desire in the Church of England for a more flexible approach to the reading of Scripture. This has led to a number of churches, some of them very large church communities, abandoning the lectionary altogether in favour of packages of readings exploring biblical issues or other matters of faith. Such churches are encouraged to use the authorized lectionary, but even those who use an authorized lectionary may need to be able sometimes to explore packages of material in a different way.

The Lectionary year is divided between 'closed' and 'open' seasons. The closed seasons are the periods from Advent to the Presentation of Christ in the Temple and from Ash Wednesday to Trinity Sunday. These periods have already been so designated in *A Service of the Word*. In these periods no departure from the RCL lectionary is allowed, and the Church will move together through the high points of the Christian year.

The rest of the year constitutes the open seasons for which authorized alternative packages may become available, but when churches would also be free to construct their own.

There need to be safeguards to ensure that opting out of the RCL be occasional, rather than frequent, even in ordinary time. Indeed, it may be that the RCL, with its semi-continuous approach to Scripture, will prove more satisfying to those who now depart from the lectionary. Equally, this freedom may help those who still feel that the liturgy is well served by a strongly thematic element to Scripture.

Weekday Lectionary

The revision of the daily office lectionary will follow with the provision for Morning and Evening Prayer. Proposals for a daily office lectionary may also include a review of the daily eucharistic lectionary in the ASB.

The Holy Days

Festivals

The eucharistic provision for festivals takes as its starting point the provision of *The Book of Common Prayer*, noting the current provision for these days by the Church in Wales, the Church in Canada and the Roman Catholic Church which have recently revised their lectionaries. Complementary office provision has been provided. The psalms and readings for Evening Prayer on the Eve are intended principally for feasts of title and patronal festivals, but may be more widely used when the minister judges it appropriate.

Lesser Festivals

The Liturgical Commission has made richer provision of Scripture for lesser festivals, and noted where a particular reading is suitable to a particular person in the calendar.

The Collects

Inter-Provincial Provision

The collect provision for Sundays and Greater Holy Days has been substantially agreed in an Inter-Provincial Liturgical Group, in which representatives of the English, Irish, Scottish and Welsh Commissions have shared in the hope of having a common set of collects, and a common translation of them, for the Anglican churches in these islands.

Principles

Each Sunday and other principal day is provided with both a collect and a post communion prayer. This will meet a real need for a variable and seasonal prayer after communion in the eucharist, and also draw more widely on the Anglican treasury of collect material. Not all the post communion prayers are specifically eucharistic, though the majority are. The collect is fundamentally a 'collecting prayer'; in the eucharist drawing together the (usually silent) prayer of the people at the beginning of the liturgy, at the office bringing to a close a period of intercessory or thanksgiving prayer. As such, though it may often be seasonal, it will not be thematic, and is not essentially a part of the Ministry of the Word or linked with the lections.

However, in the Church of England the collect has also acquired a secondary function as a 'prayer of the week' and, though the arrival of the ASB undermined this to some extent, there are still some Anglicans who desire not only to know and memorize the collect, but to associate it with a particular day or week. This use of the collect brings liturgy and spirituality together creatively and is to be encouraged.

This provision moves away from the ASB tendency to connect collect and scriptural theme. In using the RCL a choice has had to be made between attaching collects to Sunday names or to sets of lections (but not to both); the provision opts clearly for the former. Thus, for instance, the Collect for the Second Sunday after Trinity will always be the same, though the readings will change, depending not only on the stage of the three-year cycle, but also on the date on which the Second Sunday after Trinity falls in a particular year. Any attempt to relate the collect to the readings would have ruled out the attachment to particular named Sundays.

Resistance to thematic collects does not mean an arbitrary set of prayers that could have been given in any order. The provision is strongly seasonal, and intentionally so.

The Collects of *The Book of Common Prayer*

The collects of *The Book of Common Prayer* and the days on which they are used have been the starting point, departed from only with good reason. On as many days as possible, it seems desirable that Anglicans should be using the same collect, even if in slightly differing versions to accommodate the desire for both traditional and contemporary translations.

Many more of the BCP collects are used than in the ASB. In most cases BCP collects are used on their BCP day, usually as the collect of the day, sometimes as the post communion prayer. Where a BCP collect is moved, it has always been because, on its BCP day, it failed to give a seasonal emphasis of importance. Thus, for instance, some of the BCP collects for the Sundays after Epiphany and Easter have been relocated, to allow other prayers to draw out the Epiphany and Easter truths.

Now that the Sunday Next Before Advent so firmly celebrates the kingship of Christ, the 'Stir up' collect has been given as the post communion prayer, and it is also suggested as the collect at Morning and Evening Prayer throughout the ensuing week.

It has not been possible to be entirely consistent in rendering the BCP collects in contemporary English. In some cases the ASB is followed, in others the translation has gone back beyond the BCP to a Latin original. In some prayers, what some would regard as archaisms are retained. Each prayer has been looked at individually, with an eye to doctrine, to intelligibility and to rhythm, always aware that many (not all) still have an older translation lodged in their memory.

A Note also permits the use of the BCP version of a prayer where that is preferred.

Other Sources

Although there has been a good deal of criticism of the ASB collects, a great many of them are used but often with some careful rewriting.

More recent work by the Liturgical Commission in *Lent, Holy Week, Easter, The Promise of His Glory* and *Patterns for Worship* has also been drawn upon, though in all cases with revision. Material from other Anglican provinces, notably Ireland, Wales and Canada has been used. A list of sources is given.

There is also fresh writing, more in the provision of post communion prayers than of collects, and more in the Holy Days than the Seasons. In all cases, new prayers have been written by individuals, but with reworking after discussion in a group or in the whole Liturgical Commission.

Days after Festivals

Material is provided for the weekdays that follow The Presentation of Christ and Pentecost, because both these days are important cut-off points in the cycle of the seasons. They mark the end of a period of celebration. To continue to use the provision for the feast on the following days would undermine this. The same line is not taken with the Baptism of Christ (which is always on a Sunday) and Trinity Sunday; their collects and post communion prayers continue through the week, because there is no cut-off point to be marked, and the emphasis of the feast can appropriately continue through the week following.

Provision for the Holy Days

In providing collects and post communion prayers for festivals, lesser festivals, commons of saints and special occasions, the same principles as in the Seasons have been followed, though with less BCP material on which to draw.

In the collects for lesser festivals, phrases and ideas from the writings of the particular saint or Christian hero whose festival is being celebrated have been used. Sometimes (for instance, for Bishop Lancelot Andrewes) the collect shape has been stretched a little to accommodate a prayer written by the person concerned.

Sentences

There will be a need for material in the propers, other than collects and post communion prayers. It is almost certain that we shall need provision of scriptural sentences, but this work will be done when the revised eucharistic rites have been agreed and the requirements are clearer.

Traditional Language Collects

There could be a need to provide a complete set of collects in traditional language, for those wishing to follow the new calendar and lectionary, but within traditional language services. The Liturgical Commission has this work in hand.

Other Material

Material for Baptism, Healing & Reconciliation, Marriage and the Departed will be offered for consideration when the work on those rites is further advanced.

Source and Copyright Information

The copyright owners and administrators of texts included in *Calendar, Lectionary and Collects* have consented to the use of their material in local reproductions on a non-commercial basis which must conform to the terms laid down in the CBF's booklet of guidance, *Liturgical Texts for Local Use*. This is available from the Copyright Manager, Central Board of Finance, Church House, Great Smith Street, London SW1P 3NZ (tel: 0171 340 0274; fax: 0171 340 0281; e-mail: info@chp.u-net.com). A reproduction which meets the conditions stated in the booklet can be made without application or fee.

Permission must be obtained in advance from the appropriate copyright owner or administrator for any reproduction not covered by *Liturgical Texts for Local Use*. The List of Sources will help to identify the copyright holder for each text. The Copyright Manager of the CBF is able to help with addresses of the copyright owners or administrators of this material.

List of Abbreviations

ACANZP   Anglican Church in Aotearoa, New Zealand and Polynesia
ACC   Anglican Church of Canada
ASB   *The Alternative Service Book 1980*
BCP   *The Book of Common Prayer*
CPSA   Church of the Province of Southern Africa (Anglican)
CSI   *The Book of Common Worship of the Church of South India*
ECUSA   Episcopal Church of the USA
PB 1928   *The Book of Common Prayer as Proposed in 1928*

List of Sources

Every effort has been made to identify the source for each prayer. If there are any inadvertent omissions we apologize to those concerned. An * indicates that the prayer has been amended.

The First Sunday of Advent	C	ASB, BCP adapted*
	PC	*Gelasian Sacramentary*
The Second Sunday of Advent	C	BCP*
	PC	*The Promise of His Glory*, from David Silk, *Prayers for use at the Alternative Services**
The Third Sunday of Advent	C	BCP*
	PC	Westcott House, Cambridge*
The Fourth Sunday of Advent	C	*The Promise of His Glory*, based on a prayer from the Scottish Episcopal Church, *Book of Common Prayer* (also ASB Franciscan)*
	PC	ASB, adapted from Frank Colquhoun, *Parish Prayers* (author unknown)*

Christmas Eve	C	ASB, adapted from PB 1928
	PC	ACC, *Book of Alternative Services**
Christmas Night	C	ASB, translation from the *Latin Missal*
	PC	*The Promise of His Glory**
Christmas Day	C	BCP*
	PC	ACC, *Book of Alternative Services**
The First Sunday of Christmas	C	ASB, adapted from PB 1928
	PC	ASB*
The Second Sunday of Christmas	C	Church of Ireland, *Collects and Post-Communion Prayers*
	PC	ASB, BCP adapted
Epiphany	C	BCP*
	PC	*The Promise of His Glory**
The Baptism of Christ	C	ASB, based on CSI*
	PC	New composition*
The Second Sunday of Epiphany	C	ASB, adapted from CPSA, *Modern Collects* (based on CSI)*
	PC	*The Promise of His Glory*
The Third Sunday of Epiphany	C	ASB, adapted from CPSA, *Modern Collects**
	PC	ACC, *Book of Alternative Services**
The Fourth Sunday of Epiphany	C	*The Promise of His Glory*, from David Silk, *Prayers for use at the Alternative Services**
	PC	*The Promise of His Glory**
The Presentation of Christ in the Temple	C	BCP*
	PC	*The Promise of His Glory*, adapted from *The Roman Missal**
The Fifth Sunday Before Lent	C	ASB, based on PB 1928
	PC	ACC, *Book of Alternative Services*
The Fourth Sunday Before Lent	C	BCP*
	PC	BCP*
The Third Sunday Before Lent	C	BCP*
	PC	New composition
The Second Sunday Before Lent	C	ASB, new composition based on CSI*
	PC	*The Promise of His Glory*, from David Silk, *Prayers for use at the Alternative Services**
The Sunday Next Before Lent	C	ASB, adapted from PB 1928
	PC	ACC, *Book of Alternative Services**
Ash Wednesday	C	BCP*
	PC	BCP*
The First Sunday of Lent	C	ASB, adapted from BCP
	PC	Westcott House, Cambridge*
The Second Sunday of Lent	C	BCP*
	PC	BCP*
The Third Sunday of Lent	C	ASB, adapted from ECUSA, *Book of Common Prayer*
	PC	BCP*
The Fourth Sunday of Lent	C	BCP*
	PC	ASB, adapted from ECUSA, *Book of Common Prayer*
Mothering Sunday	C	Michael Perham, in *Enriching the Christian Year*
	PC	Michael Perham, in *Enriching the Christian Year*
The Fifth Sunday of Lent	C	ASB, adapted from CPSA, *Modern Collects* and Scottish Episcopal Church, *Book of Common Prayer**
	PC	ASB, new composition based on a prayer attributed to St Augustine*

Palm Sunday	C	BCP*
	PC	Church of Ireland, *Alternative Prayer Book*
Maundy Thursday	C	*Lent, Holy Week, Easter*
	PC	ASB, adapted from PB 1928*
Good Friday	C	BCP*
Easter Eve	C	BCP*
Easter Day	C	ASB
	PC	1928 PB*
The Second Sunday of Easter	C	BCP*
	PC	ASB
The Third Sunday of Easter	C	ASB
	PC	ACC, *Book of Alternative Services*
The Fourth Sunday of Easter	C	ASB, new composition based on BCP*
	PC	Church of Ireland, *Collects and Post-Communion Prayers* *
The Fifth Sunday of Easter	C	BCP*
	PC	ASB
The Sixth Sunday of Easter	C	*Lent, Holy Week, Easter* *
	PC	ACC, *Book of Alternative Services* *
Ascension Day	C	BCP*
	PC	Charles MacDonnell, *After Communion* *
The Seventh Sunday of Easter	C	BCP*
	PC	ACC, *Book of Alternative Services*
Day of Pentecost	C	BCP*
	PC	ACC, *Book of Alternative Services* *
Weekdays After Pentecost	C	BCP*
	PC	ACC, *Book of Alternative Services*
Trinity Sunday	C	BCP*
	PC	ASB, adapted from CSI*
Day of Thanksgiving for the Institution of Holy Communion	C	ASB, adapted from PB 1928*
	PC	Charles MacDonnell, *After Communion* *
The First Sunday After Trinity	C	BCP*
	PC	*The Promise of His Glory*
The Second Sunday After Trinity	C	BCP*
	PC	*Lent, Holy Week, Easter*
The Third Sunday After Trinity	C	ASB*
	PC	Janet Morley, *All Desires Known* *
The Fourth Sunday After Trinity	C	BCP*
	PC	ACC, *Book of Alternative Services* *
The Fifth Sunday After Trinity	C	BCP*
	PC	BCP*
The Sixth Sunday After Trinity	C	BCP*
	PC	ACC, *Book of Alternative Services* *
The Seventh Sunday After Trinity	C	BCP*
	PC	*Lent, Holy Week, Easter*
The Eighth Sunday After Trinity	C	BCP*
	PC	Liturgy of Malabar, in *Enriching the Christian Year*
The Ninth Sunday After Trinity	C	ASB
	PC	*Patterns for Worship* *
The Tenth Sunday After Trinity	C	BCP*
	PC	Kenneth Stevenson*
The Eleventh Sunday After Trinity	C	BCP*
	PC	Charles MacDonnell, *After Communion* *
The Twelfth Sunday After Trinity	C	BCP*
	PC	ACC, *Book of Alternative Services* *
The Thirteenth Sunday After Trinity	C	ASB*
	PC	David Silk, *Prayers for use at the Alternative Services* *

The Fourteenth Sunday After Trinity	C	ASB
	PC	ACC, *Book of Alternative Services*
The Fifteenth Sunday After Trinity	C	David Silk, *Prayers for use at the Alternative Services*, from the *Gelasian Sacramentary**
	PC	BCP*
The Sixteenth Sunday After Trinity	C	BCP*
	PC	ASB, adapted from the *Leonine Sacramentary*
The Seventeenth Sunday After Trinity	C	ASB*
	PC	BCP*
The Eighteenth Sunday After Trinity	C	ASB
	PC	Ancient prayer*
The Nineteenth Sunday After Trinity	C	BCP*
	PC	*Patterns for Worship**
The Twentieth Sunday After Trinity	C	New composition
	PC	David Silk, *Prayers for use at the Alternative Services*
The Twenty-First Sunday After Trinity	C	BCP*
	PC	New composition
The Last Sunday After Trinity	C	BCP*
	PC	ACC, *Book of Alternative Services**
All Saints' Day	C	BCP*
	PC	*The Promise of His Glory*
The Fourth Sunday Before Advent	C	David Silk, *Prayers for use at the Alternative Services*, from the *Gothic Missal*
	PC	Ancient prayer, in David Silk, *Prayers for use at the Alternative Services*
The Third Sunday Before Advent	C	ASB
	PC	ASB, adapted from CPSA, *Modern Collects**
The Second Sunday Before Advent	C	BCP*
	PC	*The Promise of His Glory*, from Charles MacDonnell, *After Communion**
Christ the King	C	ASB*
	PC	BCP*
Dedication Festival	C	ASB
	PC	Westcott House, Cambridge
The Naming and Circumcision of Jesus	C	ASB, new composition, based on BCP
	PC	New composition
Basil the Great and Gregory of Nazianzus	C	*The Promise of His Glory*
	PC	New composition
Aelred of Hexham	C	Catholic proposed national Proper for England
	PC	New composition
Hilary	C	*Celebrating Common Prayer*, adapted from ECUSA, *Book of Common Prayer*
	PC	New composition
Antony of Egypt	C	*Celebrating Common Prayer*
	PC	New composition
Wulfstan	C	Robert Jeffery*
	PC	New composition
Agnes	C	*Celebrating Common Prayer**
	PC1	*The Roman Missal**
	PC2	New composition
Frances de Sales	C	New composition
	PC	New composition
The Conversion of Paul	C	ASB, adapted from BCP
	PC1	ASB*
	PC2	ACC, *Book of Alternative Services*

Timothy and Titus	C	ASB, adapted from CPSA, *Liturgy 75*
	PC	*Patterns for Worship**
Thomas Aquinas	C	*Celebrating Common Prayer**
	PC	New composition
Charles	C	*Celebrating Common Prayer*, adapted from David Silk, *Prayers for use at the Alternative Services**
	PC1	*The Roman Missal**
	PC2	New composition
Anskar	C	New composition
	PC	*Patterns for Worship**
Cyril and Methodius	C	New composition
	PC	*Patterns for Worship**
Janani Luwum	C	New composition
	PC1	*The Roman Missal**
	PC2	New composition
Polycarp	C	*Celebrating Common Prayer*, adapted from ECUSA, *Book of Common Prayer*
	PC1	*The Roman Missal**
	PC2	New composition
George Herbert	C	*Celebrating Common Prayer**
	PC	New composition
David	C	*Celebrating Common Prayer*, adapted from Church in Wales, *Book of Common Prayer*
	PC	New composition
Chad	C	*Celebrating Common Prayer*
	PC	*Patterns for Worship**
Perpetua, Felicity and their Companions	C	*Celebrating Common Prayer**
	PC1	*The Roman Missal**
	PC2	New composition
Edward King	C	*Celebrating Common Prayer*, adapted from Lincoln Cathedral*
	PC	New composition
Patrick	C	New composition
	PC	*Patterns for Worship**
Joseph of Nazareth	C	Michael Perham, in *Celebrating Common Prayer*
	PC	New composition
Cuthbert	C	*Celebrating Common Prayer*, adapted from Durham Cathedral*
	PC	*Patterns for Worship**
Thomas Cranmer	C	New composition
	PC1	*The Roman Missal**
	PC2	New composition
The Annunciation of Our Lord	C	BCP*
	PC	New composition
William Law	C	*Celebrating Common Prayer*
	PC	New composition
Alphege	C	New composition
	PC1	*The Roman Missal**
	PC2	New composition
Anselm	C	*Celebrating Common Prayer**
	PC	New composition
George	C	Michael Perham, in *Celebrating Common Prayer*
	PC1	*The Roman Missal**
	PC2	New composition
Mark	C	ASB, adapted from BCP
	PC1	ASB*
	PC2	ACC, *Book of Alternative Services*

Catherine of Siena	C	*Celebrating Common Prayer*
	PC	New composition
Philip and James	C	BCP*
	PC1	ASB*
	PC2	ACC, *Book of Alternative Services*
Athanasius	C	*Celebrating Common Prayer*, adapted from ECUSA, *Book of Common Prayer**
	PC	New composition
English Saints and Martyrs of the Reformation Era	C	New composition
	PC	*The Promise of His Glory*
Julian of Norwich	C	Michael McLean, in *Celebrating Common Prayer*
	PC	New composition
Matthias	C	BCP*
	PC1	ASB*
	PC2	ACC, *Book of Alternative Services*
Dunstan	C	*Celebrating Common Prayer**
	PC	New composition
Alcuin of York	C	New composition
	PC	New composition
John and Charles Wesley	C	*Celebrating Common Prayer*
	PC	New composition
The Venerable Bede	C	*Celebrating Common Prayer*, adapted from Durham Cathedral*
	PC	New composition
Augustine of Canterbury	C	*Celebrating Common Prayer**
	PC	New composition
Josephine Butler	C	*Celebrating Common Prayer**
	PC	New composition
The Visit of the Blessed Virgin Mary to Elizabeth	C	ASB*
	PC	New composition
Justin	C	*Celebrating Common Prayer*
	PC1	*The Roman Missal**
	PC2	New composition
Boniface (Wynfrith) of Crediton	C	*Celebrating Common Prayer**
	PC1	*The Roman Missal**
	PC2	New composition
Thomas Ken	C	*Celebrating Common Prayer*
	PC	New composition
Columba	C	Catholic proposed national Proper for England
	PC	*Patterns for Worship**
Barnabas	C	ASB*
	PC1	ASB*
	PC2	ACC, *Book of Alternative Services*
Richard	C	New composition, based on prayer of Richard of Chichester
	PC	New composition
Alban	C	*Celebrating Common Prayer*, adapted from the Cathedral and Abbey Church of St Alban*
	PC1	*The Roman Missal**
	PC2	New composition
Etheldreda	C	New composition
	PC	New composition
The Birth of John the Baptist	C	BCP*
	PC	New composition
Irenæus	C	*Celebrating Common Prayer**
	PC	New composition

Peter and Paul	C1	ASB, based on *Leonine Sacramentary**
	C2	ASB
	PC1	ASB*
	PC2	ACC, *Book of Alternative Services*
Thomas	C	ASB, adapted from CPSA, *Modern Collects**
	PC1	ASB*
	PC2	ACC, *Book of Alternative Services*
Benedict of Nursia	C	*Celebrating Common Prayer**
	PC	New composition
John Keble	C	*Celebrating Common Prayer*, from Keble College, Oxford*
	PC	New composition
Swithun	C	Diocese of Winchester
	PC	New composition
Gregory and Macrina	C	New composition
	PC	New composition
Mary Magdalene	C	ASB, adapted from PB 1928*
	PC	New composition
James	C	BCP*
	PC1	ASB*
	PC2	ACC, *Book of Alternative Services*
Anne and Joachim	C	New composition
	PC	New composition
Mary, Martha and Lazarus	C	New composition
	PC	New composition
William Wilberforce	C	*Celebrating Common Prayer**
	PC	New composition
Oswald	C	*Celebrating Common Prayer*, from St Oswald's Church, Durham
	PC1	*The Roman Missal**
	PC2	New composition
The Transfiguration of our Lord	C	Church of Ireland, *Collects and Post-Communion Prayers**
	PC	ACC, *Book of Alternative Services**
Dominic	C	*Celebrating Common Prayer**
	PC	New composition
Mary Sumner	C	New composition
	PC	New composition
Laurence	C	*Celebrating Common Prayer**
	PC1	*The Roman Missal**
	PC2	New composition
Clare of Assisi	C	*Celebrating Common Prayer**
	PC	New composition
Jeremy Taylor	C	New composition
	PC	New composition
The Blessed Virgin Mary	C	ASB, adapted from CPSA, *Modern Collects**
	PC	New composition
Bernard	C	*Celebrating Common Prayer*
	PC	New composition
Bartholomew	C	BCP*
	PC1	ASB
	PC2	ACC, *Book of Alternative Services*
Monica	C	New composition
	PC	New composition
Augustine of Hippo	C	CPSA, *An Anglican Prayer Book*
	PC	New composition
The Beheading of John the Baptist	C	*Celebrating Common Prayer*, adapted from PB 1928
	PC	New composition
John Bunyan	C	*Celebrating Common Prayer**
	PC	New composition

Aidan	C	Catholic proposed national Proper for England
	PC	*Patterns for Worship**
Gregory the Great	C	*Celebrating Common Prayer*
	PC	New composition
The Birth of the Blessed Virgin Mary	C	*The Promise of His Glory*, from David Silk, *Prayers for use at the Alternative Services*
	PC	New composition
John Chrysostom	C	*Celebrating Common Prayer*, adapted from ECUSA, *Book of Common Prayer**
	PC	New composition
Holy Cross Day	C	ASB, adapted from PB 1928*
	PC	ACC, *Book of Alternative Services**
Cyprian	C	New composition
	PC1	*The Roman Missal**
	PC2	New composition
Ninian	C	ECUSA, *Book of Common Prayer**
	PC	*Patterns for Worship**
Hildegard	C	New composition
	PC	New composition
John Coleridge Patteson	C	New composition
	PC1	*The Roman Missal**
	PC2	New composition
Matthew	C	BCP*
	PC1	ASB*
	PC2	ACC, *Book of Alternative Services*
Lancelot Andrewes	C	New composition
	PC	New composition
Vincent de Paul	C	*Celebrating Common Prayer**
	PC	New composition
Michael and All Angels	C	BCP*
	PC	Ancient prayer, in David Silk, *Prayers for use at the Alternative Services*
Francis of Assisi	C	*Celebrating Common Prayer*
	PC	New composition
William Tyndale	C	*Celebrating Common Prayer*, from ECUSA, *Book of Common Prayer**
	PC1	*The Roman Missal**
	PC2	New composition
Paulinus	C	Catholic proposed national Proper for England
	PC	*Patterns for Worship**
Wilfrid of Ripon	C	Diocese of Chichester*
	PC	*Patterns for Worship**
Edward the Confessor	C	New composition
	PC	New composition
Teresa of Avila	C	*Celebrating Common Prayer**
	PC	New composition
Ignatius	C	G. B. Timms, in *The Cloud of Witnesses**
	PC1	*The Roman Missal**
	PC2	New composition
Luke	C	BCP*
	PC1	ASB*
	PC2	ACC, *Book of Alternative Services*
Henry Martyn	C	New composition
	PC	*Patterns for Worship**
Alfred the Great	C	New composition
	PC	New composition
Simon and Jude	C	BCP*
	PC1	ASB*
	PC2	ACC, *Book of Alternative Services*

James Hannington	C	*Celebrating Common Prayer*
	PC1	*The Roman Missal**
	PC2	New composition
Commemoration of the Faithful Departed	C	*The Promise of His Glory**
	PC	*The Promise of His Glory*, from ACC, *Book of Alternative Services*
Richard Hooker	C	Kenneth Stevenson, in *Celebrating Common Prayer*
	PC	New composition
Willibrord of York	C	Catholic proposed national Proper for England
	PC	*Patterns for Worship**
The Saints and Martyrs of England	C	Alexander Nairne*
	PC	*The Promise of His Glory*
Leo the Great	C	*Celebrating Common Prayer**
	PC	New composition
Martin of Tours	C	*Celebrating Common Prayer**
	PC	New composition
Charles Simeon	C	New composition
	PC	New composition
Margaret of Scotland	C	*Celebrating Common Prayer*, based on a prayer from the Scottish Episcopal Church, *Book of Common Prayer**
	PC	New composition
Hugh	C	*Celebrating Common Prayer*, from Lincoln Cathedral*
	PC	New composition
Elizabeth of Hungary	C	*The Roman Missal**
	PC	New composition
Hilda	C	Catholic proposed national Proper for England
	PC	New composition
Edmund	C	*Celebrating Common Prayer**
	PC1	*The Roman Missal**
	PC2	New composition
Clement	C	*The Roman Missal**
	PC1	*The Roman Missal**
	PC2	New composition
Andrew	C	BCP*
	PC1	ASB*
	PC2	ACC, *Book of Alternative Services*
Nicholas	C	G. B. Timms, in *The Cloud of Witnesses**
	PC	New composition
Ambrose	C	G. B. Timms, in *The Cloud of Witnesses*
	PC	New composition
The Conception of the Blessed Virgin Mary	C	*The Promise of His Glory*, from David Silk, *Prayers for use at the Alternative Services*
	PC	New composition
Lucy	C	*Celebrating Common Prayer*, adapted from David Silk, *Prayers for use at the Alternative Services**
	PC1	*The Roman Missal**
	PC2	New composition
John of the Cross	C	*Celebrating Common Prayer**
	PC	New composition
Stephen	C	BCP*
	PC	*The Promise of His Glory*, from *The Roman Missal*

John	C	BCP*
	PC	*The Promise of His Glory*, from *The Roman Missal**
The Holy Innocents	C	ASB*
	PC	New composition*
Thomas Becket	C	*Celebrating Common Prayer*
	PC1	*The Roman Missal**
	PC2	New composition
The Blessed Virgin Mary	C	*The Promise of His Glory*, from David Silk, *Prayers for use at the Alternative Services*
	PC	New composition
Apostles and Evangelists	C	BCP*
	PC1	ASB*
	PC2	ACC, *Book of Alternative Services*
Martyrs	C	ASB, new composition, based on PB 1928
	PC1	*The Roman Missal**
	PC1	New composition
Teachers of the Faith	C	ASB, adapted from PB 1928
	PC	New composition
Bishops and other Pastors	C1	CPSA, *An Anglican Prayer Book*
	C2	ASB, adapted from PB 1928
	PC	New composition
Members of Religious Communities	C	ASB, adapted from PB 1928
	PC	New composition
Missionaries	C	ASB*
	PC	*Patterns for Worship**
Any Saint	C1	ASB, adapted from CPSA, *Modern Collects**
	C2	New composition
	C3	New composition
	C4	New composition
	C5	New composition
	PC1	New composition
	PC2	New composition
	PC3	New composition
	PC4	*The Promise of His Glory*
The Guidance of the Holy Spirit	C1	BCP*
	C2	ASB*
	PC	ACANZP, *A New Zealand Prayer Book – He Karakia Mihinare o Aotearoa**
Rogation Days	C1	CPSA, *An Anglican Prayer Book**
	C2	CPSA, *An Anglican Prayer Book*
	C3	New composition
	PC	ACANZP, *A New Zealand Prayer Book – He Karakia Mihinare o Aotearoa**
Harvest Thanksgiving	C	CPSA, *An Anglican Prayer Book*
	PC	New composition
Mission and Evangelism	C	ASB*
	PC	ACC, *Book of Alternative Services*
The Unity of the Church	C1	ASB*
	C2	*The Roman Missal**
	PC	William Temple, in *The Promise of His Glory**
The Peace of the World	C	ASB, adapted from PB 1928
	PC	New composition
Social Justice and Responsibility	C1	Author unknown, from Frank Colquhoun, *Parish Prayers**
	C2	ASB*
	PC	New composition

Ministry (including Ember Days)	C1	ASB, adapted from BCP*
	C2	ASB, adapted from BCP*
	C3	ASB, new composition, based on PB 1928*
	C4	ASB, based on BCP
	PC1	New composition
	PC2	Charles MacDonnell, *After Communion**
In Time of Trouble	C	CPSA, *An Anglican Prayer Book*
	PC	New composition
For the Sovereign	C	ASB
	PC	BCP*

List of Acknowledgements

The publisher gratefully acknowledges permission to reproduce copyright material in this book. Every effort has been made to trace and contact copyright holders. If there are any inadvertent omissions we apologize to those concerned.

The Consultation on Common Texts: *The Revised Common Lectionary* is copyright © The Consultation on Common Texts 1992. The Church of England adaptations to the Principal Service lectionary are copyright © The Central Board of Finance of the Church of England, as are the Second and Third Service lectionaries.

Cambridge University Press: Extracts adapted from *The Book of Common Prayer* (1662), the rights in which are vested in the Crown in the United Kingdom, are reproduced by permission of the Crown's Patentee, Cambridge University Press.

The Central Board of Finance of the Church of England: *The Alternative Service Book 1980*; *Lent, Holy Week, Easter*, 1986; *The Promise of His Glory*, 1991; *Patterns for Worship*, 1995; *The Prayer Book as Proposed in 1928* (additions and deviations); new compositions by the Liturgical Commission of the General Synod of the Church of England are copyright © The Central Board of Finance of the Church of England.

Anglican Church in Aotearoa, New Zealand and Polynesia: *A New Zealand Prayer Book - He Karakia Mihinare o Aotearoa*, © The Church of the Province of New Zealand 1989.

General Synod of the Anglican Church of Canada: Based on (or excerpted from) *The Book of Alternative Services of the Anglican Church of Canada*, copyright © 1985. Used with permission.

Catholic Bishops' Conference of England and Wales. Used with permission.

International Commission on English in the Liturgy: The English translation of the collects and the post communion prayers from *The Roman Missal* © 1973, International Committee on English in the Liturgy, Inc. All rights reserved.

General Synod of the Church of Ireland: *Alternative Prayer Book*, 1984; *Collects and Post-Communion Prayers*, 1995. Reproduced with permission.

Church of the Province of Southern Africa: *An Anglican Prayer Book 1989* © Provincial Trustees of the Church of the Province of Southern Africa (includes material from *Modern Collects*, 1972 and *Liturgy 75*, 1975).

Episcopal Church of the USA, *The Book of Common Prayer* according to the use of the Episcopal Church of the USA, 1979. The ECUSA Prayer Book is not subject to copyright.

Church in Wales Publications: *The Book of Common Prayer for use in the Church in Wales*, Vol.1, 1984. Used with permission.

Cassell plc: C. L. MacDonnell, *After Communion*, 1985; David Silk (ed.), *Prayers for use at the Alternative Services*, 1980; revised 1986; The Society of St Francis: *Celebrating Common Prayer: A version of The Daily Office SSF*, 1992 are copyright © Mowbray, an imprint of Cassell.

HarperCollins *Publishers* Limited: Martin Draper (ed.), *The Cloud of Witnesses*, 1982. Copyright © G. B. Timms.

Hodder and Stoughton *Publishers*: Frank Colquhoun (ed.), *Parish Prayers*, Hodder and Stoughton, 1967.

Oxford University Press: *The Book of Common Worship of the Church of South India*. Used by permission.

The Very Reverend Robert Jeffery

Canon Michael McLean

Janet Morley: *All Desires Known*, SPCK, 1992.

Michael Perham (ed.): *Enriching the Christian Year*, SPCK/Alcuin Club, 1993.

The Right Reverend Kenneth Stevenson

The Diocese of Chichester: *The Chichester Diocesan Calendar*

The Dean and Chapter of Durham Cathedral

St Oswald's Church, Durham

The Warden and Fellows of Keble College, Oxford

The Dean and Chapter of Lincoln Cathedral

The Dean and Chapter of the Cathedral and Abbey Church of St Alban

Westcott House, Cambridge

The Diocese of Winchester: *Local Saints and Heroes of the Faith*, 1984